*The University of North Carolina*
*Social Study Series*

# TEXTILE UNIONISM
# AND THE SOUTH

# THE UNIVERSITY OF NORTH CAROLINA
## SOCIAL STUDY SERIES

UNDER THE GENERAL EDITORSHIP OF HOWARD W. ODUM. BOOKS MARKED WITH *
PUBLISHED IN COÖPERATION WITH THE INSTITUTE FOR RESEARCH IN SOCIAL SCIENCE.

# TEXTILE UNIONISM
# AND THE SOUTH

BY

GEORGE SINCLAIR MITCHELL, Ph.D.

*Instructor in Economics in*
*Columbia University*

CHAPEL HILL
THE UNIVERSITY OF NORTH CAROLINA PRESS
1931

# PREFACE

THIS is a study of a long, and some think useless, agitation. Cotton mill operatives in the South are here shown to have been sharers in a spasmodic trade union movement reaching clear back to the days of the Knights of Labor. Of the many strikes, however, only two or three can be said to have been even partially successful, and until the outbreak of strikes in 1929, there was little evidence that the turmoil had had much direct effect on wage scales and working conditions, even through public opinion or legislation. Naturally, though, all this tale of troubles has not been followed through by the author without some belief in the effectiveness, for good or for evil, of the agitation studied.

The use of the movement, one has come to see, is largely educational. I confess to a sympathy with the efforts of the mill people to organize, and with the efforts of the northern unionists to do the organizing. At first my feelings were stirred by the fraternity of the labor movement in the South. Here was sacrifice, altruism, fellowship, opposing a species of tyranny. When the study was for the most part done I went to England for several years, and spent a good deal of time in Lancashire, where the greatest cotton industry in the world has been built up. As I investigated the early history of the union movement there, I saw that the character of the laboring class in that country had been deeply influenced by its attachment to the principle of organization. The roots of democracy among the North of England workingmen draw sustenance from the trade unions and the non-conformist churches. The unions taught restraint, the slowness

with which great changes are accomplished, and in micro-
cosm they initiated the humblest into the methods of public
meetings, the points by which to judge proffered leadership,
the conduct of continuous and pushful organizations. Had
not those lessons been well learned, it is doubtful if the ter-
rible distress of Lancashire in the last decade would have
been endured without bloodshed.

Something of this work of democratization seems to me
the lasting benefit of trade unionism. If the unions can secure higher wages and better conditions, or can materially
aid the Southern cotton manufacturers in restoring the industry to complete and successful operation, much is gained.
Probably unionism will never be permanent until economic
profit for the workers who share in it has been demonstrated.
Nevertheless, even the spasmodic organization which this
study recounts has not been without its influence in tauten-
ing the intellectual muscles of the mill people.

The South, as in the past, is still an authoritarian society.
The cotton industry has reproduced for its owners the position of power held by the masters of plantations. The company town concentrates initiative in the mill management;
and, though many mills have responded with valuable pat-
ronal arrangements, designed often to instill self-reliance,
the mill village system has not yet found its own antitoxin.
A wider franchise than obtained in *ante-bellum* days has
made retrieving by the manufacturers of the old planters'
political dominance a matter of finesse; but political, and
nowadays social, power are the manufacturers', nevertheless.
The South, even more than the rest of America, relies upon
wealth for its guidance.

It is the plain white people of the South, though, who

will decide the great issues that face that region. Authority cannot dictate an acceptable adjustment of race relations; nor can it ensure that the Southern people, now rapidly regaining a place of importance in the nation's councils, shall show themselves informed and temperate. The solution of the grinding problem of Southern agriculture awaits initiative among the farmers, not among 'their political representatives. Just behind the democratization of the whites, so necessary to genuine progress, lies the certainty that a similar movement must occur among the blacks.

The trade union offers at this stage an entering wedge of democracy, at any rate for the white factory laborers. Organization in achieving power usually learns responsibility. It would appear to be the part of wisdom for the South to welcome an instrument that promises aid in leavening the great class of mill people. Unionism once accepted in the mills would probably overflow into organization among other groups. It is not too much to expect, as the consequence of any established factory unionism, a reversal of the whole trend of socio-economic power in the South.

G. S. M.

Richmond, Virginia
December, 1930

# CONTENTS

# TEXTILE UNIONISM
# AND THE SOUTH

# CHAPTER I

## THE NORTHERN UNIONS

TEXTILE unionism in the United States has always been extremely weak. Between 1900 and 1915, from fifteen to twenty-five thousand is a liberal estimate of the average number of union operatives. In the war years membership climbed to something over 150,000, but since 1922 it has been stable at a figure little above thirty thousand. At the most, about four per cent of the 1,100,000 textile workers in the country are organized. This diminutive membership is split among a dozen separate unions, the largest of which controls less than two-thirds of the organized workers. Most of the union operatives are relatively skilled workers; unionism has reached among the unskilled masses only when crises have forced them into hasty combinations, abandoned as soon as work was resumed. Very little energy has gone toward constructive dealing with the larger problems of the industry; the unions have been skeleton battle units for resistance and aggression on wages and hours.

Savage, in his *Industrial Unionism in America,*[1] in accounting for the feebleness of textile unionism, listed as causes the size and complexity of the industry, the prevalence of the craft spirit, the conservatism of the leaders of the largest union, the low degree of skill required, the large proportion of women and children, the low wages, and the predominance of immigrant labor. Of these the last four are the most important. The lack of skill lessens the pressure which can be placed upon employers, makes it easy to shift from one section of the industry to another, and is partly

[1] P. 252.

responsible for a low intelligence among the workers and for difficulty in securing capable leadership. The women in the industry have been less a hindrance to the unions than might be supposed, since many of them have expected to continue in the mills for long periods, and in strikes, at least, they have supported the unions as well as the men; but the younger workers have been unorganizable.

The low wage level has meant that unions had a choice of a fluctuating membership signed for very small dues or of a fairly stable membership of the more skilled workers able to pay higher contributions, and for most of them the latter basis has been chosen. Added difficulties are the remarkable dispersion of the industry even in the older New England and Middle States centers; the frequency and severity of trade depressions brought about by changes of fashion; and the disastrous effects of competition within the country. Undoubtedly, however, the root cause of the weakness in the Northern section of the industry is the fact that it has drawn its labor in the main from immigration. Since the Civil War, when the native American labor finally withdrew from the larger New England mills, the predominating groups have been successively, British, French Canadians, and East and South Europeans, with a sprinkling of Germans, of Portuguese, and of other nationalities. Except among the English, Irish, and Germans, unionism has had very little success. The racial groups have been mixed indiscriminately in the big textile cities, and their own animosities and the barriers of language and religion have kept them disorganized.

But these factors do not entirely account for the failure of the textile unions to build substantial memberships. The explanation lies partly in the intermittent feuds between the unions themselves. The textile organizations fell into separate camps almost from the beginning; the geographical spread of the industry, the tradition and power of the separate crafts, and the issue of federalism versus centralization made this inevitable. Confusion based on these factors has been increased by the entry of extreme left-wing agitation under a succession of fleeting organizations, mainly among the more recent immigrants. The disputes between these sections have prevented collective action toward improvement of labor standards and have diverted the energy of the unions from the task of organizing the body of non-union labor below them.

If these are the obstacles, there remain a few circumstances that favor the union movement. Most branches of the industry are still highly competitive. The six thousand odd separate textile manufacturing establishments in the country represent nearly that many independent corporations, each with a constantly varying degree of ability to resist union attacks; so that the organizations have many chances to gain a foothold. Another more doubtful advantage is the ease with which strikes can be enlarged. A parade and a few speeches will often bring wholly unorganized workers tumbling out of their mills, to lend their weight for a brief while to the workers who first expressed their grievance in a strike. But the spreading strike is a two-edged weapon—more often than not the necessity for supporting the new recruits cripples the first strikers, the original grievance is lost sight of in wider demands, and the collapse blackens the whole adventure. But the employers' knowledge that strikes spread probably gives union committees some leverage in negotiation.

The roots of the modern textile unions do not go back much beyond the sudden growth of the Knights of Labor in the middle 'eighties. The New England mill girls had carried on a vigorous ten hours' agitation and had taken part in a series of turnouts in the 'forties and 'fifties, but they had failed substantially to improve conditions and had left the field to the incoming Irish and English immigrants.[2] The only group among these who kept alive something of the Lancashire unionism almost from the first were the cotton mule spinners of Fall River. These men were in combination in 1850; by 1858 they had formed an association of New England locals; after the Civil War they had become strongly organized again in 1876, and by 1890 they had finally revived the inter-local association. The spinners had helped the Fall River weavers and card-room hands to combine in 1875, but it had taken fifteen years or more and the assistance of the Knights to form a strong body of English-model locals of these crafts, the slasher-tenders, loom-fixers, beamers, and others in Fall River and New Bedford.[3] These cotton craft unions, drawing their strength from the more skilled workers in the two finer goods cities, believing in strong local treasuries and loose federal organization, and already in the 'nineties winning a recognized standing with their employers, were the first of the four union groups in the industry to emerge.

In the Middle States the brief period of organization

[2] Norman Ware, *The Industrial Worker, 1840-1860,* ch. VII.

[3] History of the Fall River Cotton Mule Spinners Association, Handbook of the Association, 1894, pp. 79-91. *Proc.,* International Spinners Union, 1917, p. 6.

under the Knights of Labor left behind a number of scattered craft unions, several of which have lasted through until now. The Knights made little progress in the textile industry, except about Philadelphia and in Fall River, until 1885, the year of the great uprising of unskilled labor. When in 1886 the union began to fall apart, the various textile crafts, already separated into textile and silk trades assemblies, began to withdraw as independent "national" unions. The jackspinners had gone out in 1883 and the carpet weavers in 1885; they were followed afterwards by nationals of silk workers, upholstery ʃweavers, hosiery knitters, and others. The lace operatives organized in 1893 on a basis of English unionism. These various independents had not the cohesiveness of the New England cotton unions, since they were formed for the most part to protect crafts in distinct branch-industries, but the stronger ones persistently refused to take part in any of the amalgamations, and in time they came to have a certain collective interest in preserving their status as separate unions.

The first of these amalgamations was the National Union of Textile Workers, organized in 1891 by the American Federation of Labor, and in some respects the prototype of the present United Textile Workers. The union drew together one or two of the New England cotton unions and a few weaker crafts from the Middle States, but most of the organizations refused to come in. In 1895 a Socialist victory within the National Union of Textile Workers alienated the New England cotton men, who withdrew and left the National Union to drift. It began to revive in the last year or two of the century, when the American Federation of Labor was bringing the union new recruits gained in its

Southern campaign; but it had never been taken seriously by most of the textile unions, and its preaching of industry-wide unionism and its plea for the suppression of craft nationals had had little effect. It was this failure of the first attempt at amalgamation, plus the A. F. of L.'s natural wish to place the conduct of the newly-started Southern movement in the hands of an inclusive textile union, that led to the shift of forces in 1901.

While the N. U. T. W. was limping and the Middle States independents were slowly strengthening themselves, the New England cotton unions were forming a loose federation of their own. The New Bedford Weavers, who had led the secession from the N. U. T. W. in 1895, between that year and 1900 drew the weavers, carders, loom-fixers, and slasher-tenders of Fall River and New Bedford, the mulespinners, and a handful of cotton locals elsewhere in Massachusetts, into an American Federation of Textile Operatives.[4] This body, distrusting the leadership and methods of the N. U. T. W., petitioned the A. F. of L. for a separate cotton-workers' charter, but the A. F. of L. backed the industrial principles of the old amalgamation and persisted in its efforts to bring the two groups together. A series of conferences between representatives of the larger unions worked out a general plan of fusion, and a convention for a new amalgamation finally met in Washington in 1901.

The compromise agreed upon was that in forming a new, chartered textile union the principles of inclusive jurisdiction and centralized authority should be constitutionally provided for, while dues to the central treasury should be fixed

---

[4] Albert Hibbert, in *American Federationist*, Nov., 1902, p. 873; *Proc.*, A. F. T. O., 1900.

at the low figure to which the cotton men were accustomed
in their own Federation. This arrangement brought the
American Federation of Textile Operatives and the National
Union of Textile Workers into one union, but it drew little
support from the fringe of independents. The Paterson
silk-workers, the lace operatives, and a number of Philadelphia unions remained outside, and the mulespinners did no
more than affiliate. To this combination of weak Southern
locals, Middle States silk, hosiery, and carpet workers, and
New England cotton craft unions, the name United Textile
Workers of America was given, the name being suggested,
it is said, by one of the Southern local officials.[5]

From the formation of the U. T. W. until 1915 the
unions drifted steadily back toward the position of 1900.
The U. T. W. was in its early years controlled by the Fall
River and New Bedford locals, but in 1903 they took the
first step toward losing control by placing at the head of the
union John Golden, a former Lancashire spinner. Golden
by training should have shared the opinions of the Fall River
localists, but as president of the United Textile Workers he
set himself to build a centrally strong union. He gradually
forced up the per capita tax, regardless of the withdrawal of
union after union in New England. The Fall River and
New Bedford weavers went out in 1903 and 1906, more
Fall River locals in 1908, and the woolsorters in 1909. In
order to avoid destruction, the union in 1907 divided itself
into two sections, one paying a relatively high tax and re-
ceiving in return strike and death benefits, and the other
keeping to a low quarterly contribution. The division of
membership, while it satisfied the Massachusetts cotton men

[5] C. McDaniel, interview, Augusta, Ga., July 3, 1924.

who remained in after 1908, was a constant gall to the growing body of locals which paid on the higher scale. The organizing wave which swept over the industry after the Lawrence strike of 1912 gave these locals a majority in the conventions, a majority which they were prepared to use to destroy the 1907 arrangement. The fine goods men tried once more to persuade the "industrial" section that stability and expansion lay in accentuating craft lines and in decentralizing finances and authority;[6] but in 1914 a ruling for equal contribution was finally passed. The result was a last secession that took away the mulespinners, some scattered cotton locals, and a body of full-fashioned hosiery knitters. The fine goods unionists then proceeded to revive the federation which they had dissolved when they entered the U. T. W. in 1901.

The prosperity of the war years seemed to justify Golden's belief that nothing had been lost in scraping off the "barnacles on the textile union movement." In 1914 the U. T. W. had grown from the 10,000 members with which it started only to some 18,000. In 1916 it took in more than this last number as new members and reported its whole membership at 32,000. From then it climbed rapidly to a peak of over 100,000 in 1920.[7] Much of this new member-

---

[6] "These oracles of the trade union movement will never get the idea out of their heads that all you have to do is to simply transplant the British idea and form of trade unionism into this country and everything will run along O. K. Unions of special crafts will spring up like mushrooms, and the problem of organizing the textile workers of this country will be solved." (President Golden, in *The Textile Worker*, Aug., 1915, p. 3.)

[7] Leo Wolman, *The Growth of American Trade Unions*, p. 110. Proc. U. T. W., 1914, p. 22; 1916, pp. 17, 118; 1919, pp. 30, 43; 1920, p. 77. Thomas F. McMahon, History of the United Textile Workers of America, *Workers' Education Series*, No. 2.

ship came from branches of the industry which before the war had hardly been reached by the union. In the South the desultory activity that had been kept up after 1912 gave way in 1919 to a widespread campaign that planted locals all through the Piedmont and carried forty or fifty thousand operatives into the union. In the Northern mills the union was largely responsible for gaining the forty-eight hour week in 1919. But activity on this scale was the product of inflation and national unrest. Depression in 1920, the Southern strike in 1921, and the New England strike in 1922 clipped the reported membership back to 30,000—the figure at which it has stayed ever since.

After the final secession from the U. T. W. which led to the revival of the old alliance of the cotton craft unions, the latter body had until recently a fairly stable existence. In 1916 its membership was optimistically put at 14,000.[8] The war years and the contrast of its methods with those of the U. T. W. gave it a small harvest of new locals. "The form of National organization in the textile industry," wrote the President in 1919, "which gives the greatest confidence to the rank and file of the workers, encourages and keeps organization together, is that which makes conditions liberal enough to allow local unions to create a substantial treasury of their own, and be in a position to give a reasonable support to the members of their own local union when emergencies arise. By the adoption of such a policy many of the dangers which now tend to weaken the power of the organized textile labor movement would be averted."[9] When the expansion was at its greatest, the union enlarged its theoretical juris-

[8] *Proc.*, National Amalgamation of Textile Workers, 1916, p. 9. (The name American Federation of Textile Operatives was resumed in 1920.)
[9] *Textile Operatives' Journal*, May, 1919, p. 2.

diction to include workers in other branches than cotton, but the depression prevented any real trial of strength between the Federation and the United Textile Workers.

From 1922 till 1927, membership was consistently given as 12,000. The backbone of the union continued to be its English and Irish leadership, but with the shutting off of immigration and the rapid Americanizing of the Fall River and New Bedford populations, the immigrant groups came to fill fully half its ranks. The Federation remained active in promoting protective State legislation and it drew support from the favored position which its conservative policy brought it with the employers. The strike in New Bedford in 1927 lost it all of the locals of that city, since these bodies found it desirable to gain the support of the general labor movement by affiliating with the United Textile Workers. The Fall River unionists remained loyal to the American Federation of Textile Operatives, though that body now includes little more than Fall River and locals in ten or a dozen southern New England towns. Membership is probably under 5,000.

Neither the United Textile Workers nor the American Federation of Textile Operatives has succeeded in lessening by much the number of smaller independents. Most of them have been built around localized skilled crafts, often in small branch industries whose connection with the larger textile industry is not close, and many of them have long since attained a satisfactory relationship with their employers. The largest of them and the leader of the group at present is the Amalgamated Lace Operatives, with locals mainly in Pennsylvania. Philadelphia had until recently five independents: the Brass Bobbin Winders, the Tapestry Carpet

Weavers, the Upholstery Beamers and Twisters, and the Power Loom Fixers. Officials of the U. T. W. give the combined membership of these unions and the lace operatives as about 4,000. Outside Philadelphia are such unions as the Machine Printers, the Friendly Society of Engravers, the Mechanical Workers' Union of Amsterdam, a remnant of the National Woolsorters' and Graders' Association, and the now diminutive Amulet Association of Jackspinners. At present these number less than 1,000 members together. The independents are a fluctuating group, their number shifts with the fortune of strikes, and a gradual absorption of them into the U. T. W. seems to be in process.[10] The Tapestry Carpet Weavers and a local of Wilton weavers joined the U. T. W. in 1928. In the campaign for a new unification during 1922-23 most of the independents, with the A. F. T. O., entered a loose association fostered by the left-wing Amalgamated Textile Workers and named the Federated Textile Unions of America. This body functioned during the 1922 strike in New England and facilitated the conferences on amalgamation, but the A. F. T. O. and some of the other unions have since withdrawn and the Federated, though it continues to exist, has become a paper alliance.[11]

These three sections of the movement, the U. T. W., the A. F. T. O., and the older independents, have all relied for their stable membership upon the older immigrant strains— indeed none of them except the U. T. W. has ever had even

[10] Cf. Robert Dunn, *American Labor Year Book,* 1921-22, pp. 155-162, for a description of the independent unions and the conflict with the U. T. W. at the period of expansion.

[11] Its proceedings were reported with those of the A. F. T. O. A good account is given by Gladys Palmer, Labor Relations in the Lace and Lace Curtain Industries in the U. S., in *U. S. Bureau of Labor Statistics, Bulletin 399* (1925). *Cf.* Savage, p. 273.

temporary success with the more recent immigrants. The class-conscious bias of many of these workers has perhaps been as great a deterrent to their joining the regular unions as the difficulties of language and nationality. At any rate, the unions which have from time to time enlisted considerable numbers of them have done so with the aid of more or less left-wing propaganda. The first stirring of the masses was done by the I. W. W., which began in 1907 or 1908 an intermittent agitation that culminated in the great Lawrence strike of 1912. Though the older union succeeded in discrediting the I. W. W. leadership, the movement was vigorous until the later war years, and among the Paterson silk workers a section of the union remained alive until 1919. During the war period, however, the unskilled in the main either trusted to economic forces to gain them wage advances or in small groups found room for themselves in the standard unions, though little was done to make the scheme of organization more acceptable to the immigrant workers; on the contrary, tax rates were rising, officials were losing touch with their membership in proportion as it rose, and the patriotic emphasis upon "American" unionism was alienating a markedly proletarian labor force. Thus it was that when the 1919 tide of unrest swept the industry, no union existed into which the unskilled would readily flock.

To fill this gap the short-lived but remarkably successful Amalgamated Textile Workers was formed. This union arose out of the Lawrence strike early in 1919, in the course of which the unorganized strikers found themselves in dispute with the few members of the U. T. W. in the city, and were taken under the protection of the Amalgamated Clothing Workers and guided by three or four outside labor sympathizers. The experience gained in organizing the immigrant workers there was promptly made use of in spontaneous strikes in Passaic and elsewhere, and before the end of the year the new A. T. W. had taken in some 50,000 members. The union was completely democratic in structure and Socialist in its phraseology. It was soon deep in a war of abuse with the U. T. W., but until the beginning of the long depression it appeared to have little prospect of needing Golden's proposed epitaph, "Here lies the twin-brother of I. W. W.'ism." Short time and wage reductions broke its front in 1920, and, though it rallied for the 1922 New England strike, it dwindled rapidly to its disappearance early in 1925.

During the boom years the Amalgamated had a feeble rival in the shoots that came down from the One Big Union movement in Canada. This body led a scattered agitation mainly in New England and Canadian mills, but its appeal was likewise stopped by the depression, though it controlled a section of the Lawrence workers in 1922.

A left-wing union that has survived is the Associated Silk Workers, with a membership largely among ribbon and hat-band weavers in Paterson. The ultra-democratic form of organization is carried over from the impetus of the Amalgamated and the old Paterson I. W. W., but the union no longer greatly differs from the other independents. Though it has refused to join with them in the Federated Textile Unions of America, it has at times considered fusion with the U. T. W. It has claimed a membership of 4,000 or more since its beginning.

Though the continued depression in the Northern industry has prevented the survival of much of the 1919 unionism among the new immigrants, it was adequately shown in the communist-led Passaic strike of 1926 that the basis of class-conscious unionism in the industry had by no means disappeared. The attempt of the United Textile Workers to include the organizations which survived the Passaic strike ended in fiasco. The New Bedford strike in the next year showed the same Communist influence. In 1928, when the Communist movement determined to form its own unions, surviving nuclei in Passaic and Paterson served as a basis for a new National Textile Workers' Union. Though the organization strangely confounds political and economic agitation and surpasses most of its fellow textile unions in the fluctuation of its membership, it continues to offer opposition to the other unions in the industry, and has been active in widely separated parts of the country.

Unfortunately for the progress of unionism in the industry, this fourfold division of forces has many times led to quarrelsomeness. The minor craft unions have lived peacefully one with another, since their jurisdictions have seldom overlapped, but the U. T. W. and the unions composing the American Federation of Textile Operatives have been in more or less open conflict for the last twenty-odd years, both of these unions have fought the left-wing organizations, and the U. T. W. has carried on a running fight with the small independents ever since it was founded. The root of much of the dispute is the inclusive jurisdiction given the U. T. W. in its A. F. of L. charter. With the prospect of a single industry-wide organization constantly before it, the United Textile Workers has prosecuted its claim to the full. The minor unions, usually based upon key crafts in a small branch industry, have not unnaturally wished to keep intact the bargaining machinery which they have built up, and have seen little advantage in substituting for their own treasuries a system of contributions to a general fund notoriously slender and subject to many calls only distantly related to their own craft interests.

If these minor unions kept their separate organization they were constantly being cried down by the U. T. W. as "outlaws" and "traitors to the great American labor movement," and occasionally they were attacked. They have been deprived of assistance in disputes not only from large numbers of organized textile workers, but from the A. F. of L. unions in general. The same position has been taken by the U. T. W. in regard to the A. F. T. O. unions, but with them the excuse for local autonomy is less valid because their interdependence, with the rest of the cotton unions, at any rate, is clear, and it is difficult to show that the U. T. W. officials are not sufficiently familiar with the requirements of the Fall River operatives to enable them to care for their interests. The dispute between these two unions was especially disastrous to the union movement, because the fine goods mills, in which most of the members of the A. F. T. O. are employed, are traditionally important in wage fixing for the whole cotton industry, and the frequent disagreements as to requests for advances or as to the point at which resistance to reductions should be made, has caused much confusion and bitterness. The relentless enmity between the U. T. W. and the left-wing unions has probably hurt the U. T. W.'s membership rolls more than those of the newcomers. Much of their propaganda has been directed at the supposedly undemocratic methods of the A. F. of L. union, and that union's antagonism has seldom lost the left-wing unions any support.

The whole tangled situation decidedly weakens unionism in the industry. It diverts attention from the problem of organizing, makes all the unions seem worthless to the outsiders, foredooms strikes to weak support and poor discipline, and alienates employers.

The bearing upon the movement in the South is that the division of the unions has meant that the whole effort of extending organization to that region has been left to the resources in ability and money of one of the unions, representing less than two-thirds of the organized workers in the industry. The United Textile Workers is the only union which has had the support of the A. F. of L., and, in consequence, has been the only union which could draw upon the outside labor movement for help with the Southern work. The claim to inclusive jurisdiction and the policy of centralization in that union have kept alive an enmity with the other unions; those unions have not only been disinclined to help with the Southern activity of the U. T. W. but they have been prevented from pushing locals of their own into the region (in the few cases where branches of their particular crafts have been established in the South), by the certainty that any such locals would be bitterly attacked by the U. T. W.

In so far as the disputes of the Northern Unions have lessened the effectiveness of their work among the unskilled, they have further hampered the extension of unionism to the South, since the more skilled operatives who are at present unionized are those who feel the pressure of Southern competition least, and who are therefore under less incentive to reach into the competing field than are the unskilled, but un-organized, workers in medium-count mills.    Nevertheless, the unions outside the U. T. W. have all an indirect interest in propagating organization in the South, and, if the quarrel with the chartered union could be settled, it is probable that, with the exception of the National Textile Workers' Union, they would contribute substantial help in the Southern movement.

All the unions have recognized the weakening effects of disunity and most from time to time have gone half-heart-edly into efforts at amalgamation.    The leading part in the early movements was played by the A. F. of L., which was responsible alike for the old National Union of Textile Workers and for the second fusion which formed the United Textile Workers of America.    In the period from 1901 to 1915, when the U. T. W. was perfecting its centralized ad-ministration, little more than abuse of the independents and seceders came from that union; and in the war years, with membership in all the societies mounting rapidly, each union was sufficiently pleased with its own success to make con-solidation seem unnecessary.    The bitterness of the mutual abuse increased as the unions grew stronger, until in 1919 and early 1920, when the U. T. W., the A. F. T. O., and the vigorous Amalgamated were all bidding for the same textile workers, the prospect of a joining of forces seemed very distant.

The depression brought an about-face almost at once. The Amalgamated Textile Workers busily organized the Federated Textile Unions of America, purposely to seek some compromise with the U. T. W.    Meanwhile the U. T. W.

had been working on two tacks. It prosecuted with the A. F. of L. its case for the forcible entry of the chartered unions of mulespinners and lace operatives into itself; but those unions preferred to allow their charters to be recalled late in 1919 rather than accept the U. T. W.'s conditions. In 1921, however, it met with more success in negotiations with a large section of the full-fashioned hosiery knitters, which was induced to rejoin the loyal knitters' local with which it had broken in 1914 and enter the U. T. W. again; this time as part of an autonomous American Federation of Full-Fashioned Hosiery Knitters, affiliated to the A. F. of L. through the U. T. W., and paying, in addition to the tax collected by its own officers, the standard tax to the U. T. W. Though it was the high wages of these skilled operatives which enabled them to accede to this arrangement, the admission of an intact craft federation was a break in the U. T. W.'s former stiff prohibition of such subordinate societies (if the affiliation of the mulespinners from 1901 to 1914 be not considered), and as such made it seem more probable that reasonable compromises would be offered to the other independents. This was followed up in the return of the New Bedford locals, which were given a degree of autonomy that would never have been countenanced in 1919.

At the present time the tendency seems to be decidedly toward the winning over of the independents by the U. T. W. Conferences with this end in view have been held frequently since 1923, and at each U. T. W. convention new accessions have been reported. It is probable that the remnant of the A. F. T. O. will not be able to stand by itself. Several Philadelphia independents are well disposed toward the U. T. W., and the Associated Silk Workers, hammered by the National Textile Workers' Union (Communist), may fall in with the American Federation of Labor union. The problem of disunity is, however, still far from being solved.

# CHAPTER II

## THE EARLY MOVEMENT IN THE SOUTH

ALTHOUGH in the older centers of the industry the union movement has been so weak, it has found resources for a good deal of intermittent effort in the Southern mills. The activity there has fallen into four or five periods, separated by years when almost nothing was done. The first hints of organization came in the later 'eighties, when the declining Knights of Labor made a feeble attempt to organize in the new Southern mills. During the 'nineties, or at least until 1898, agitation disappeared completely. But at the end of the century the tinder left by the Knights caught fire, and for four years, from 1898 to 1902, the noise of unions and strikes spread through the region, from Georgia to Virginia and back again. The new textile union in the North burnt its fingers in a strike at Augusta in 1902, and withdrew any active assistance until 1912, so that another period of silence followed this second agitation. But in 1913 a dramatic strike in Atlanta started a series of local disturbances in Georgia, South Carolina, and East Tennessee that lasted through 1918.

With the end of the war, Southern labor shared the sudden forward push of labor elsewhere, and in the mills of North Carolina tens of thousands of workers went into the union. Strikes for shorter hours popped up all through the State, and several employers undertook not to discriminate against union operatives. But when sharp wage cuts followed the stagnation that came in 1921, the pressure of the newly-powerful operatives was too great for the Northern officials to hold back. The Southern workers called for a show-down fight, and got it. At the end of 1921 hardly a single active local survived in the whole region. Inactivity continued until late 1927, when new efforts at organization in the South were put on foot, to be followed by the series of strikes in the spring and summer of 1929, and after that by a general organizing campaign.

The events of all four periods of activity—1886-1890, 1898-1902, 1913-1921, and 1928-1930, reveal the background of difficulties which the union movement faces in the South. The Knights of Labor, who inaugurated the modern labor movement in the textile industry, found strength before their expiration to push a feeble wing into the South. In 1886, the year which witnessed the commencement of the Knights' decay in the Northern industrial areas, a series of "assemblies" was founded in the larger Southern cities. From them the movement quickly spread into the rural districts, so that by the summer of 1888 seven Southern States had two hundred or more active assemblies.[1] As a "labor" union the Knights included every sort of producer of which the region could boast; its agitation reached even to a few groups of colored workers.[2] Typical town assemblies were those at Columbia Factory, North Carolina, where the members were "chiefly mill hands and farmers, although nearly every trade, religious denomination and political party" was

[1] Two hundred and eight Southern assemblies (35 in Virginia, 64 in North Carolina, 10 in South Carolina, 27 in Georgia, 25 in Tennessee, 33 in Alabama, and 14 in Mississippi) were among the 3,350 odd whose votes in a referendum were recorded in the *Journal of United Labor,* May 19-June 30, 1888.

[2] *Ibid.,* Feb. 18, April 7, June 9. *Morning News,* Savannah, Ga., Oct. 21, 1886.

represented, and at Thomasville, Georgia, with a "membership composed of brick-masons, carpenters, plasterers, painters, shoemakers, blacksmiths, merchants, preachers and common laborers."[3]   Most of such strength as the Knights had, however, came from the poorer farmers.  Of 112 assemblies in Alabama, Georgia, North and South Carolina which wrote in to the weekly journal in 1888, 47 said that their members were mainly farmers, three had mostly cotton mill hands, and 62 either had a mixture of farmers and artisans or did not state their composition.[4]

After 1888, the most active year, the artisan membership rapidly dropped away, leaving the agricultural portion to vanish in the early 'nineties.

Probably not much of this organization under the Knights reached the new cotton mill operatives.  No effort was made to unionize the mill people as a separate group; but here and there considerable numbers of these workers seem to have come under the influence of the Knights. Augusta, Georgia, where the mills were old and the village population settled, had a long Knights of Labor dispute in 1886.   The manufacturers there organized against the Knights and countered a strike in one mill with a lockout of some four thousand operatives.   Three thousand of this number the Knights claimed as members.[5]   Two months of the lockout, with irregular local administration of relief funds from headquarters, brought the operatives back without the wage increase they had demanded; but the employers agreed with a committee to abolish the "petty tyrannies com-

[3] *Ibid.*, Feb. 25, March 3.
[4] *Ibid.*, Jan. 7-Dec. 28.
[5] *Proc.*, Knights of Labor, 1886, p. 46.

plained of," reinstate the workers locked out, remit rents for the idle time, and to arbitrate all future difficulties.[6]

Next year, at Fishing Creek, South Carolina, a representative from the Knights found that the mill had "discharged all of its employees because they were members of the Knights of Labor," but he could effect no settlement.[7] In 1888, disturbances connected with the Knights' movement occurred at Cottondale, Alabama, Greenville, South Carolina, and Maryville, Tennessee. At Roswell, Georgia, in 1889, an organizer in adjusting the discharge of several Knights found "nearly the entire force of the factory . . . Knights of Labor," and claimed to have put through a no-discrimination agreement.[8] Doubtless other disputes occurred.

A good deal of objection to company stores found expression through the Knights, and local leaders protested against the low wages which the army of mill recruits made inevitable. But it is not to be concluded that a concerted textile agitation appeared. The assemblies, even when they contained mill operatives, were small, widely separated, and of fleeting existence. Most cotton mill centers probably were entirely unreached. The result, after the Knights had gone by, could have been little more than a planting of the notion of combination.

From the disappearance of the Knights of Labor after 1890 until nearly the end of the century, the Southern mill workers were left alone. It was not until they had begun to show signs of a union revival of their own that organizers again came down.

[6] *Morning News,* Savannah, Ga., Aug. 8-Nov. 5, 1886.
[7] *Proc.,* K. of L., 1887, pp. 1414, 1438.
[8] *Ibid.,* 1889, p. 20.

Twelve years after the defeat in Augusta, a new dispute there threw open the whole question of Southern unionism. When a wage cut was announced late in 1898 a portion of the operatives under the leadership of Prince W. Greene, of Columbus, hurriedly formed local unions. When Greene's followers applied for affiliation with the American Federation of Labor they were directed to join the purged but weak National Union of Textile Workers. The A. F. of L., concerned over the threat of backward Southern conditions to labor standards elsewhere, was just then preparing for a general campaign in the South. It sent into the region organizers instructed to give particular attention to the movement in the cotton mills, and from 1898 to 1901 continued to support the mill unions with leadership and money. The National Union of Textile Workers played a secondary rôle, though all the locals joined it. Its tax was low, its Northern membership was very small, and it had no support from the other unions in the industry. The Southern workers inside it were surprised to find themselves holding the majority vote. Prince Greene was president from 1898 to 1900, and secretary-treasurer from 1900 until the merger with the United Textile Workers; and during most of the Southern activity the union's head office was at Columbus.

Membership in the four years of activity was at no time large. Most locals probably counted their paid-up members by scores instead of by hundreds. It was considered remarkable that Rock Hill had 150 charter members, Macon 200, and Greensboro 225.[9] In strikes, of course, membership grew. Augusta, after the 1898-9 strikes, claimed 3,500

[9] *American Federationist*, Sept., 1900, p. 289; June, 1900, p. 178.

members,[10] and Danville, at the time of the 1901 strike, had 1,400.[11] The whole N. U. T. W. in 1900 estimated its membership at 5,000, though it made a much higher claim for the next year. Probably the Southern membership was never much above 4,000, but a much larger number than this passed through the union. As for Southern locals, the highest number reported in the union's conventions was ninety-five. Nothing like this many could have been active at any one time, but examination of the various union publications during the period yields the names of at least thirty-six towns in the five leading mill States in which one or more textile locals were actually formed, and of many others in which organizing activity was carried on. The Augusta district boasted nineteen locals in 1901.[12]

For the first few months the union confined itself almost entirely to Augusta. It carried organization belatedly to workers in Atlanta, who had two spontaneous strikes in 1898,[13] and next year it was responsible for a loomfixers' strike in a Columbus mill, where the fixers, protesting against extra work, were locked out and non-union men put in their places.[14] The locals in Augusta had been formed to resist a threatened wage cut. When the cut came weavers at one mill went out and were "speedily joined with great cheering by hands in the other departments."[15] Enough operatives left their mills to close eight of them, but four were able to resume almost at once with the reduced wages. A month

[10] Ibid., Feb., 1898, p. 24. C. McDaniel, interview, Augusta, Ga., July 3, 1924.
[11] Proc., National Union of Textile Workers, 1901, p. 47.
[12] Ibid., p. 125.
[13] Proc., National Union of Textile Workers, 1898, pp. 3-6.
[14] American Federationist, Nov., 1899, p. 255.
[15] Chronicle, Augusta, Ga., Nov. 22, 1898.

after the strike began three more mills locked out their employees sympathetically. This brought the whole number out of work to 4,000. Two or three weeks broke what resistance remained and the operatives went back under the low wage, but with "unofficial" terms calling for some sort of union recognition, no discrimination against strikers, sale of fuel at cost, and "an agreement about the rents accumulated during the strike."[16]

While the Augusta strike was in progress the union had held out as bait to the manufacturers a promise that it would carry organization into the Carolina mills and bring the scales there up to the Augusta level. By the end of 1900 the A. F. of L.'s organizers had spread a thin network of locals in North and South Carolina. Lockouts occurred at Greenwood, Abbeville, and at Bath,[17] and in North Carolina there were a feeble strike at Durham, lockouts at Greensboro and Fayetteville,[18] and a long dispute in Alamance County.

In this instance the union had been in the county four or five months when weavers at one mill were discharged for refusing to work under an overseer whom they disliked. Three Haw River mills were struck at once. A few days later all the mills in the county posted notices that after a given date only non-union operatives would be employed. When the notices went up workers gradually left the mills until after three weeks several thousand were out, with sixteen mills closed. Financial support was weak and many

---

[16] *Ibid.*, Jan. 27, 1899. *Cf. American Federationist,* Nov., 1899, p. 159.
[17] *Proc., N. U. T. W.,* 1900, p. 22; *American Federationist,* Feb., 1900, p. 4.
[18] Holland Thompson, *From the Cotton Field to the Cotton Mill,* p. 192; *Proc., N. U. T. W.,* 1900, p. 29.

of the locals ran into debt.   The union busily sent off hands
to new mills.   After six or seven weeks resistance collapsed,
and some locals disbanded, many unionists left, and a few
were evicted.   Holland Thompson, mentioning the dispute,
said "no disorder occurred."[19]   It was a complete defeat for
the union and little was heard of organization in North
Carolina for the rest of the period.

From Burlington and Haw River, North Carolina, the
center of activity shifted to Danville, Virginia.   The usual
work day in the Carolina mills was eleven or twelve hours;
in Danville it was twelve.   Late in 1900, a local there took
up the agitation for ten hours.   The mill, whether or not
influenced by the union's resolutions, announced that it
would work the short day from January 1 to April 1, when
the schedule would go back to eleven hours for the summer.
The union used the breathing space to prepare for resistance
to the eleven hour day.   When April 1 came, President
Gompers of the American Federation of Labor was in Danville to encourage the operatives.   The mill, after consideration, posted a reasoned argument against assumption of a
further competitive disadvantage.   The local "voted to remain out until the ten hour day was secured."   The strike
drifted into the hand of local politicians two weeks after it
was declared, and the mills were soon able to resume on their
own terms.   A remnant only of workers held out some weeks.
longer.[20]

Broken in the Upper Piedmont, the union shrank back
to its Augusta stronghold.   In November, 1901, the Na-

[19] Thompson, *ibid.*, p. 194.   *Cf. News and Observer*, Raleigh, N. C.,
Oct. 5-Dec. 27, 1900; *Proc.*, International Union of Textile Workers,
1901, pp. 32, 34, 112-113; *American Federationist*, Dec., 1900, p. 388.
[20] *Proc.*, I. U. T. W., 1901, pp. 41-51, 127.

tional (then the International) Union of Textile Workers
had entered the new United Textile Workers of America.
The change had shaken loose the old Southern leaders of the
I. U. T. W., so that the Fall River officials were in charge,
and the dispute gave them their first experience in the
Southern field.  The council of the Augusta locals, feeling
itself strong enough to try for a ten per cent wage increase,
selected one large mill where the weavers had an additional
grievance over the measurement of yardage, and put in a demand, accompanied by a threat to strike.  Three days after
the strike began the manufacturers in the Augusta district,
organized ever since the 1886 lockout of the Knights of
Labor, closed down.  About 7,000 workers, with perhaps
12,000 more direct dependents,[21] were involved. The United
Textile Workers, having closed the strike, ordered an assessment and began the collection of funds.  T. M. Young, who
visited Augusta during the lockout, found a well-ordered
commissary system, a tent colony strung along the Savannah
River, and a holiday-making population of farmers and fish-
ermen, apparently not in great distress.  The U. T. W., in
spite of lagging response to the assessment, raised some
$10,000.  After seven weeks the mills resumed, though the
one originally struck still had only a small force.  Some of
the strikers were removed with evictions, others returned to
work, and seventeen weeks after the strike was declared the
U. T. W. officially surrendered.[22]

Though the spread of organization under the N. U. T.
W. was thus wholly unsuccessful in forcing wage changes

[21] *Chronicle,* Augusta, April 9, 1902.
[22] *Proc.,* U. T. W. of A., 1902, pp. 10, 17; C. McDaniel, interview.
*Chronicle,* Augusta, Mar. 29, May 23, 1902; T. M. Young, *The American
Cotton Industry,* pp. 78-86.

upon employers or in reducing the hours of labor, it did have some effect in awakening public opinion in the region to the absence of protective labor legislation. The A. F. of L. subsidized the agitation largely with the intention of beginning a movement for such legislation, and saw to it that committees of union textile workers waited upon State Assemblies and pressed for passage of bills restricting child labor, limiting weekly hours, and prohibiting wage payments in truck. These efforts hastened the beginnings of protective legislation in the region.

For ten years after 1902 the United Textile Workers gave little serious attention to the South. The policy was the result partly of the union's experience in the final Augusta strike, partly of the absence of any signs that unions could be easily revived in the region, and partly of the composition of the U. T. W. itself. For the union disasters in Alamance County and Danville, the old N. U. T. W. had been responsible; in Augusta the Northern officials experienced for themselves the cost and difficulty of a Southern adventure. The men at the head of the U. T. W. carried a stout tradition of English craft unionism; with them the way to retrieve defeat was to cling to organization. When the Augusta unionists melted away, so that the city was completely unorganized a few weeks after the strike was over, the general union perhaps thought them deserving of the discipline of self-help. Also, in the organization of the U. T. W., the skilled craft men had come out on top; their policy was to strengthen the unions of the upper level of cotton workers before much was done with the unskilled and with the South. The low tax rate and the series of secessions prevented progress even in this. Moreover, even if the failure of the N. U. T. W. movement had not definitely turned the Southern workers against unionism (and probably it had), it would have required more money than the U. T. W. could raise to revive the agitation.

The A. F. of L. having formed the U. T. W. in part to relieve itself of the problem of the South, no longer felt direct responsibility to finance a campaign. But the Northern officials did not abandon the South without a final testing of the Southerners' temper. John Golden, then vice-president of the U. T. W., was sent through the region in 1903. He produced a faint revival in the Horse Creek Valley in South Carolina, but in the Carolinas generally he found the workers either lukewarm or afraid to organize. For eight or nine years after his trip no U. T. W. agent visited the region.

Although the U. T. W. did nothing active to encourage organization in the South, a few weak unions were formed, usually by persons locally interested. In 1906 one or two diminutive locals sent dues up again from the Horse Creek Valley; two locals were chartered at Columbia, S. C., in 1907 (one of the mills locked out the unionized loomfixers and so broke the union);[23] and another was formed at Henderson, North Carolina, in 1910. Outside the Piedmont a local or two was placed in nearly every Southern textile State, but nowhere did the unions last more than a few months. The evidence accumulated that unionism would not grow in the South without persistent effort on the part of some outside body.

The U. T. W.'s apparent apathy toward the South was gradually sloughed off in 1912 and 1913. In 1912 an or-

---

[23] *Proc.,* U. T. W. of A., 1907, p. 26.

ganizer met some success in forming locals at Danville and Lynchburg, and at Knoxville signed a large body of workers in a mill which offered no opposition to the union movement. In the same year the A. F. of L. convention at Atlanta left an impetus to organization. Next year, when the Knoxville members resolved "that the time is now ripe for an organizing campaign in the Southern States,"[24] and undertook to share the expenses of an organizer for the region, the union agreed to try its chances in the South again. The new attitude coincided with the increase in the U. T. W.'s high-tax membership, which put the more aggressive locals in control. Golden, who had all along preached Southern unionism, thus found his hands loosed. When a start was made in the South the bitter Atlanta strike in 1914 gave the movement wide advertisement. After 1915 the union profited from war expansion, bringing with it absorption of much of the surplus labor, rising wages, and a premium upon uninterrupted production. In these circumstances the union's policy was to encourage whatever groups could be organized to apply for immediate improvement in conditions. It found itself involved in a long chain of strikes, and its energy went into fighting out situation after situation rather than into building a network of unions. The activity was mainly in the lower Piedmont and East Tennessee; North Carolina resisted attacks until 1919.

In Georgia, at the start of this third period of activity, the long dispute in Atlanta overshadowed two or three smaller ones. A brief spontaneous walkout in one of the Atlanta mills, in October 1913, had failed to remove the

[24] *Ibid.*, 1913, p. 70.

working rules of which the operatives complained.[25]  While
the grievance there simmered, Augusta was being organized.
When a handful of Augusta loomfixers struck against new
shop regulations, they were joined after a month by 500
more hands from the same mill, but were brought back two
weeks later on the company's terms.[26]  Next year a strike
typical of many in the South occurred at Rome.  By the
union's account, soon after the local was organized officers
and active members were paid off.  The mill refused a conference and posted an anti-union notice.  More members
either struck or were discharged.  With a little help from
the U. T. W. and the State Federation of Labor, the usual
"splendid fight" was kept up for two months, when the members drifted into other mills, no settlement having been
reached.[27]

Meanwhile a U. T. W. agent had organized some of the
workers at Atlanta and had met the discharge of union committees and the refusal to grant a conference with a strike.
The union demanded recognition, the reinstatement of the
committeemen, and the consideration of the complaints of
the year before: poor housing, the withholding of a week's
pay, fines for absence, and a pass system for leaving the factory.  The long array of grievances and the dramatic appeal
of a tent colony for the eighty-five families whom the company evicted, gave the union good talking points in an appeal
for funds, and it aired to the full its views of Southern conditions.  About nine hundred were on the strike list for a
time.  Violence seems not to have been serious; the union

[25] *Textile Worker*, Dec., 1913.
[26] *Proc.*, U. T. W. of A., 1914, p. 34; *Chronicle*, Augusta, Dec. 30,
1913-Jan. 18, 1914.
[27] *Proc., ibid.*, 1914, p. 97.

reported only two arrests, and thought the magistrate severe when he fined the strikers $50 for "simple assaults."[28]  In spite of a picket line the mill gradually filled, and though some of the strikers hung on for a year the strike was broken a few weeks after it was called.  But defeat did not injure the union's propaganda; from Atlanta the sense of grievance spread.

For the next two years the union was busy with a campaign and a series of strikes in South Carolina.  In 1914 Greenville had furnished a startling spectacle of organization in a strike led by the Industrial Workers of the World.  The I. W. W., on the decline of a wave of agitation in the textile industry that had reached its height in 1912, had gained a foothold in one of the larger mills in Greenville early in 1914.  In July, on a dispute over lost time, it brought out 750 workers.  South Carolina blinked when a parade carried the red flag down the village streets.  Readiness to confer with committees and the raising of the race issue brought the operatives back in a week, prepared to conform to the mill's rules.[29]  Next year, when a U. T. W. organizer went into Greenville, it took a good deal of explaining to clear away "misunderstanding"; but the excitement under the I. W. W. probably did not hurt the U. T. W.'s chances.  Late in 1915 an outside observer wrote that "in the vicinity of Anderson there are some 1,000 members of the union, and it is said that the mills in Greenville County show a larger aggregate membership."[30]

[28] *Proc., ibid.*, 1914, pp. 35, 36, 98; 1915, p. 36; *Textile Worker,* Aug., 1914, pp. 23, 24; *Constitution,* Atlanta, May 20-June 9, 1914.

[29] *Textile Manufacturer,* Charlotte, July 16, 1914; *Southern Textile Bulletin,* July 23, 1914; *Textile Worker,* June, 1915, p. 15; *The State,* Columbia, July 11-18, 1914.

[30] *The State,* Columbia, Oct. 28, 1915.

The U. T. W.'s agitation brought a weak strike in another Greenville mill. In the autumn, when a local had been placed in the factory, the officials gave the hands an address which "confused the workers somewhat";[31] but later seventy-five weavers left their looms in protest against discharges said to have been discriminatory. Within a few days enough of the force had withdrawn to close the mill. Evictions involving about a hundred persons were put under way, with orders that they be temperately enforced. A petition circulated among the villagers to request reopening of the mill showed that three-fourths desired to return to work but were "taking no stand against the union." After three weeks, when the mill had started, a remnant of the strikers engaged in an early-morning "rookus" on the picket line, with the death of one operative as the result. Throughout the strike, and especially in the trial of the men involved in the outbreak of violence, the mill showed a high degree of tolerance.[32] The president considered the later events of the strike as a progressive effort on the part of the better residents of the village to rid themselves of a rowdy element.[33]

Meanwhile a dispute was in progress at Anderson, in the next county. There something less than six hundred workers left their mills after the discharge of a union committee. A picket line that hindered the shipment of cloth and used obstructionist tactics annoyed the employer, and a volley or two of pistol shots into the air made some disorder. After ten weeks Federal mediators, assisted by a representative of Governor Manning, effected a settlement under which the

[31] *Proc.*, U. T. W. of A., 1916, p. 91.

[32] *The State*, Columbia, S. C., Oct. 26, Nov. 10, 27, 1915; *Proc.*, U. T. W. of A., 1916, p. 92.

[33] B. E. Geer, interview, Greenville, S. C., July 11, 1924.

company reëmployed all the strikers except ten, and deferred collection of rentals due for the period of the strike. The men who were refused employment urged acceptance of the terms, and were supported by the local until they found other work.[34]  The following summer, operatives at two more Anderson mills presented a demand for a 10 per cent increase, backing their request with the argument that even larger increases had been granted in the North.  (The fact that the mills were Boston-owned increased the force of the plea.)

The management refused the increase, but admitted the prosperous state of the factories and offered a bonus conditioned upon steady work for four months in the future. The union wanted higher wages with no strings attached. It struck both mills, one three weeks after the other.  The local claimed as members two-thirds of the seven hundred people out.  Again picketing hindered the company from carrying out non-manufacturing activities, and threats were freely used, but actual disturbance was small.  State and Federal mediation failed because, if the union is to be credited, the employers were "unwilling to have the employees say they received an increase in wages through the unions."[35] When the strike had dragged along three or four months the mills began eviction proceedings, but the delay of a sheriff to turn the operatives out forced the Governor to send troops to uphold the court orders.[36]  Six days afterward both mills had opened, with the gates protected by artillerymen.  Working forces were gathered with difficulty,

[34] *Proc.*, U. T. W. of A., 1915, p. 47; *ibid.*, 1916, pp. 90-91. *The State*, Columbia, Nov. 3-30, 1915; *Textile Worker*, Dec., 1915, p. 4.
[35] *Proc., ibid.*, 1917, p. 47.
[36] *Proc., ibid.*, p. 95; *The State*, Columbia, Aug. 9-Nov. 16, 1916.

as the union was active in sending families away from the village. The defeated union cherished a resentful belief that it had deprived the mills of their best help.

Smaller strikes were occurring at Westminster and Columbia, South Carolina, and in Anniston, Alabama. A three weeks' lockout following discharges of union members ended the Westminster local.[37] At Columbia a strike in one mill was settled through a State conciliator, with the workers claiming small advances.[38] At Anniston an unorganized and successful one-day protest against a preferential arrangement with a store in which the mill superintendent was interested, brought a U. T. W. organizer, who proceeded to unionize several of the mills. At one the process entailed a shut-down for three weeks, when the workers were taken back, the union reported, as members.[39]

South Carolina at the end of 1916 may have turned against the union; at all events the Piedmont strikes in 1917 and 1918 were in Georgia. At Cedartown a small knot of mulespinners furnished one of the few disputes in the South led by a union on the outs with the United Textile Workers. A new local of the International Spinners' Union in the late spring negotiated for a 10 per cent increase. Later two committeemen were discharged. Though the general officers advised conference with the employer, the twenty-five mulespinners and seven back-boys went out without it. The Fall River officers granted the local strike pay, but nine weeks later when the secretary went down he found that the money had been loosely spent and the strikers who remained were

[37] *Proc., ibid.,* 1916, p. 59.
[38] *Ibid.,* pp. 58-61.
[39] *Ibid.,* p. 59.

inactive. Reinstatement of the committeemen could not be effected, and though the mill was unsuccessful in attempts to secure an injunction and damages, the strike ended in defeat.[40] The other 1917 strike at Griffin, Georgia, likewise began with the discharge of union members. It was rapidly enlarged by a "volunteer, sympathetic walkout" which closed two mills and reduced the forces in five others. The union busied itself in sending hands off to other mills, to farms, and to the new employments thrown open by the war, until several hundred had left the town. The U. T. W. claimed a small wage increase in the end, with what comfort its members could extract from the tacit recognition of "the right of the workers to work unmolested with their union card."[41]

The period of scattered disputes in the Lower Piedmont ended with the unionization of the Columbus, Georgia, operatives in 1918. Early in the spring a U. T. W. organizer, visiting the city during a lockout led by a representative of the Georgia Federation of Labor, fell heir to the union agitation already begun. When the lockout could not be settled directly with the manufacturers or through a Federal mediator, the workers were sent back into the mills instructed to deny union membership. Minor appearances of discrimination later were boldly met. In one mill that was making army cloth, pressure from a government inspector was ingeniously used to stop discharges. The excitement of the year came when a spinning company turned off twenty-five unionists and the local closed it with a strike of some five hundred workers. Deputies sent to keep order after the fir-

---

[40] *Proc.,* I. S. U., 1917, pp. 10, 12, 42, 43; *Times,* Chattanooga, June 30, 1912.

[41] *Proc.,* U. T. W. of A., 1917, pp. 58, 61; *Journal,* Atlanta, Sept. 2, 1917; *Constitution,* Atlanta, April 14, 1918.

ing of shots from within or around the mill were roughly handled by the strikers (the Irish organizer reported that one deputy "was met five minutes later six squares away hurrying home, on account of his wife being sick"), with a consequent visit to Columbus of United States troops, Home Guard companies, and martial law. The union people continued their meetings across the Chattahoochee River, in Phoenix City, Alabama. In the end, representatives of the War Labor Board negotiated a settlement which contained some elements of victory for the workers. Readjustment of the 50 per cent bonus was promised, grievances were to be reported through shop committees, and the men originally discharged were taken back before the body of the strikers entered the mill. The union committees later took up the apportionment of the bonus and secured the transfer of two-thirds of it to straight wage. In October, new increases in piece rates in one mill were reported as having come through a union demand. During the agitation some 4,500 workers were said by the union to have been signed as members.[42]

Minor disturbances in the same year occurred at Atlanta, where the originator of the Columbus agitation was active in another lockout and at Graniteville, South Carolina, where the Columbus U. T. W. agent unionized some of the operatives and with difficulty warded off a strike.[43]

Early in 1919 the union's activity in the South underwent so many changes that it is as well to regard the years from 1913 to the end of 1918 as forming a distinct period in the development of the movement. Perhaps the chief characteristic of these five years was the confinement of

[42] *Proc., ibid.,* 1918, pp. 49-36, 91, 92; *Constitution,* Atlanta, April 14, 1918; *Chronicle,* Augusta, Aug. 16, 20, 1918.
[43] *Ibid.* pp. 54, 55, 56.

unionism to the immediate vicinity of the places in which disputes concentrated the union's force. The union did not have enough outside financial assistance to enable it to throw a network of organizers through the region. Possibly its strategy was to give its entire attention to each strike situation, in the hope that one substantial victory would make the union's position stronger than many quick failures. As for membership, it signed the workers by hundreds, and sometimes, as at Greenville and Anderson and Columbus, by thousands in the particular places in which it happened to be engaged; but at no time did the movement show a disposition to extend beyond the areas within easy reach of the organizers who were leading strikes.

In the whole period only about forty local unions were chartered in the region, and several of these were in East Tennessee. Positive gains that the union could claim were in these years, as in 1898-1902, very few. Wages were climbing hand over fist. Probably the scattered agitation hurried their rise in a good many Georgia and Carolina cities, but in only one or two minor instances did the union gain any immediate success. Hours of labor, for all the union claimed, were unaffected by the strikes. It is highly probable, however, that the rumors of unionism contributed something to the growth of the welfare movement as a defense tactic of the employer.

A factor in making local agitations possible was labor scarcity. Two other conditions aided the union. The employers showed little evidence of concerted action against the union. Their policy may have been to keep the union talked about as little as possible (certainly in 1917 and 1918 news items about strikes in some towns were compressed or omitted as a patriotic duty), in the belief that even a partly sleeping dog had better be let lie. At all events, no considerable anti-union propaganda appeared.    The other factor which made the union's task lighter was the readiness of other labor bodies to aid in the disputes.    Cotton mill strikes were to many unionists a new appearance; failure had not recurred often enough to make it seem inevitable, and central labor unions and State federations voted strike relief without misgiving.

Early in 1919 the union agitation in the mills burst through whatever conditions had kept it localized and suddenly began to flow all through the Upper Piedmont.    In that year the South shared to a remarkable and largely unchronicled extent in the wave of unrest.    Southern towns and cities were flung abruptly into strikes of almost every sort of workmen they contained.    The street railwaymen were out in a whole series of towns, railroad shopmen were out late in the year, and in North Carolina unionism thrust itself forward in the tobacco and furniture industries.    In East Tennessee the metal industries had long disputes.    The unrest was partly the result of the breaking-down of isolation and the new knowledge of wages and hours elsewhere in the country; in the cotton mills it took the form of protest against the long weeks and a general demand for the transfer of the war-time bonuses to straight wage.    In encouraging these demands the U. T. W. played a leading rôle, but even if it had not offered itself as a vehicle for the rapid growth of unionism in 1919, it is highly probable that some other means would have been used to express the unrest of the operatives.

The spark which set off the train of disputes was the

union's strategic demand for the forty-eight hour week. Late in 1918 it set February 3, 1919, as the day upon and after which textile workers should refuse to work the long week. Though it was not expected that much success would be had in the South, the union's members there were nevertheless urged to stand with the Northern workers, and when the appointed day came Southern papers carried news of a simultaneous walkout in Columbus, Georgia, the Horse Creek Valley in South Carolina, in Chattanooga, Tennessee, and at Sherman, Texas. In the first two places the workers strongly resisted a return to the old hours, and the knowledge that at the lower end of the Piedmont "eight hours" was being fought for must have hastened the outbreak of organization in the Carolinas. Columbus was in a fever of agitation all through the first half of the year. For a time after the 1918 dispute the U. T. W. agent reported most of the mills as willing to confer with local committees, but late in January of 1919 discharges in one mill induced the union to withdraw 750 workers from it. This number was joined on February 3 by nearly the entire operative population of the city.

Two-thirds of the seven thousand who were out were not entitled to strike benefits and it was agreed that the sums due should be shared alike in the form of commissary supplies. Attempted mediation failed. A good deal of disorder occurred on both sides. When one strike-breaker was badly "cut up," the strikers accepted an offer of non-prosecution of the men arrested in return for withdrawal of the picket line. With the pickets taken off, the mills filled rapidly and two months after the walkout began the employers were reporting that 80 per cent of the people were back at work.

When the dispute had thus been won for the mills, and most of the remaining strikers had voted to return to work, the manufacturers of the district announced a reduction of hours to fifty-five per week, to conform to the recent reduction in South Carolina and in other Georgia mills. One mill, in accepting its old operatives, demanded that they destroy their union cards.[44] Though the union had to stretch language to claim even a partial victory in the lockout, it found it possible to nurse the locals back to nearly their old strength. In May, when endorsement had been received for another strike in one of the mills, a union meeting just off the company property was fired into by a group of company supporters (including a number of foremen and overseers), with the death of one man and the wounding of several others as the result.[45] Later, when the union put in a request for a wage increase, it was partly granted, leaving the organizer to contend that unionization had secured in some of the mills a shorter week with nearly the old pay.

In the Horse Creek Valley in South Carolina, the forty-eight hours demand was responded to by numbers of the workers in two mills and the next day 2,000 people were locked out. The union opened a supply room and collected funds from nearby trade unionists. Fifteen families, ordered to leave company houses, were advised "to stay where they were until they were carried out." Although during the lockout the cotton manufacturers of South Carolina re-

---

[44] *Proc.,* U. T. W. of A., 1919, pp. 52-57; *Daily Times,* Chattanooga, Feb. 22, 1919; *Chronicle,* Augusta, Feb. 22, 28, 1919; *Observer,* Charlotte, Feb. 1, 4, 1919, *Daily News Record,* New York, March 3-June 4, 1919.
[45] *Proc., ibid.,* p. 56; *Constitution,* Atlanta, Ga., May 22, 23, 1919.

duced the hours of labor from sixty to fifty-five,[46] the locals refused an offer of reëmployment on this schedule with discharge of the workers ordered evicted, and the dispute was not settled until some weeks after the reduction of hours.[47]

Later in the year an angrily conducted strike occurred at Macon, Georgia. The local trades council, having organized some of the mill operatives, called in a U. T. W. representative. After six locals had been formed the principal firm began discharging union leaders. The organizer, believing the mill wished to force a strike, advised delay, but the union members were impatient and in two weeks drew out 2,000 operatives from five or six mills. The demands were recognition and the eight-hour day. After three weeks, during which the strikers on the picket line had indulged in occasional rough handling of the people returning to work, the mill had succeeded in getting a small staff on the machines. The union charged that the company was using a larger proportion of colored workers than usual. A truck carrying non-union operatives was fired into and two Negro women in it were killed and several others wounded. Twenty-four strike leaders, including the organizer, were arrested. With the union leaders in jail, the company announced a resumption of work. The strikers, advised by other trade unionists and given the approval of their leaders, agreed to return, though many who had been concerned with the rioting were refused reëmployment, and in some mills, at least, the men taken back were required to "give up all outside association." The union officers were released without prosecution, and the U. T. W. agent was instructed to

---

[46] *Cf. Southern Textile Bulletin,* July 24, 1919.

[47] *Proc., ibid.,* 1919, pp. 49, 52, 59; *Textile Worker,* Feb., 1919, p. 418; Mar., 1919, p. 466; *Chronicle,* Augusta, Ga., Feb. 4, 1919.

leave Macon and Georgia.[48] The displays of temper which this strike brought out discredited the organizer who had led the Georgia movement since 1918, and in consequence weakened the union's hold all through the lower Piedmont.

Though the eight hours agitation in Columbus and Graniteville prepared the way for the spread of organization in the Carolinas, the immediate beginning there was a hastily organized but partly successful strike in Charlotte. Late in February some of the mills in the northern part of the city removed a 30 per cent bonus and reduced working time to four days a week. The operatives appealed to labor sympathizers in the city, who called in organizers from the U. T. W. Fifteen hundred workers promptly joined the union. In retaliation the North Charlotte mills locked out all union members, and one company had a branch mill in Huntersville follow suit when its operatives were organized. After about four months union committees met the manufacturers and adjusted the stoppage on an open shop basis, with reinstatement without discrimination, a fifty-five hour week with the old sixty hours pay, incorporation of bonuses in the wage, and free house rent for the duration of the lockout. Meanwhile about 500 operatives in a chain of mills in East Charlotte had joined a U. T. W. local and 1,500 had been locked out. In ten weeks these mills resumed under a verbal agreement based upon that used in North Charlotte.[49]

The sudden success in Charlotte and the strikes which

[48] *Proc., ibid.,* 1919, pp. 57, 58; *Observer,* Charlotte, Aug. 25, 27, 1919; *Constitution,* Atlanta, Aug. 23, Sept. 17, 1919; *Daily News Record,* New York, Sept. 9, 22, 1919.
[49] *Proc., ibid.,* 1919, pp. 85, 86. *Observer,* Charlotte, March 4, 9, June 10; *News and Observer,* Raleigh, N. C., May 30, June 2, 9; *Southern Textile Bulletin,* June 5, 1919, p. 9; J. F. Flowers, interview, Charlotte, N. C., Aug. 14, 1924; Marvin Ritch, interview, *ibid.*

came later made a wide demand for organizers. The U. T. W. brought down more from New York, the A. F. of L. sent in agents, and local labor men busied themselves in the campaign. In North Carolina the membership grew by bounds. Before September, 43 locals had been chartered in the State. In many mills the operatives were organized 70 or 80 per cent; in a few, such estimates as 95 per cent went unchallenged. The union claimed that in two months in the middle of the year, 16,000 workers had applied for membership.[50] President Golden declared in the autumn that 40,000 were carrying paid-up cards in North Carolina, and one of the organizers put the outside number for South Carolina membership at 5,000.[51] Figures like these were rounded on the favorable side, perhaps by a good many thousands, but they indicate a substantial wave of organization.

The other important disputes, at Concord and Belmont, North Carolina, Rock Hill, South Carolina, and Albemarle, North Carolina, all ended with some provision for open shop conditions. When the Concord operatives were unionized, the principal employer followed the Charlotte tactics and locked out some 2,000 people. The union agents extended organization to mills owned by the same company at Kannapolis, six miles away, and with the leverage of a threat to strike there induced the company, after three and a half months, to confer with union representatives and approve their issuance of a statement that the mills in both towns would be run on a fifty-five hour week with the sixty hours pay, without discrimination against union members, and

[50] *Textile Worker,* June, 1919, p. 114.
[51] *Proc., ibid.,* 1919, p. 92.

with meetings with mill employees to discuss grievances, and that back rents would be cancelled.[52] At Belmont the lockout was again used and a number of families were served with eviction papers. In spite of what the union considered to be over-zealous policing by Gaston County officials, the operatives were able in the end to negotiate for substantially the same conditions granted in the earlier disputes.[53] In Rock Hill the union in one mill demanded a 25 per cent wage increase and withdrew five hundred workers when a conference was refused. A few days later nearly as many again left two mills nearby, but returned in two days, accepting an earlier offer of 5 per cent increase in wage. The mill first struck remained closed for ten weeks, when mediation by South Carolina officials resulted in a settlement calling for reinstatement without discrimination, changes in wages which the union called a "general levelling up," and transference of the bonus to regular wage. The issue of recognition in this instance was evaded by stipulation that the mill would confer only with representatives from among its own employes, and that the local union should have no outside affiliation.[54] At Albemarle, when the mills closed for the usual week's rest, the recently unionized operatives at most of the plants refused to return when the week was over, unless formal recognition of the union were granted. Employers at a leading mill delayed reply on the ground of the absence of the company's president.

[52] *News and Observer,* Raleigh, April 15, May 19, June 2, 5; *Times,* Concord, N. C., June 4; *Observer,* Charlotte, June 11, 1919; *Proc., ibid.,* 1919, pp. 59, 87, 88.

[53] 10 *Proc.,* U. T. W. of A., 1919, pp. 89, 90.

[54] *Proc., ibid.,* 1919, pp. 88, 89; *State,* Columbia, Aug. 9-14; *Observer,* Charlotte, Aug. 7, 12, 14, 1919; *Daily News Record,* New York, Aug. 11, Sept. 30, 1919.

When the strike had been in progress a month, police attempted to disarm pickets.  A small riot ensued, and militia companies were sent in for several days to keep order.  Union agitators were arrested.  A fortnight later terms were reached which provided for future dealing with committees on some questions, reinstatement on an open shop basis, and instalment payment of back rentals.  It was carefully stipulated, however, that "the foregoing basis of adjustment . . . shall not be construed as a recognition by the mills of collective bargaining."[55]

Smaller disturbances, brought on by demands for recognition or disputes over working conditions, occurred at McAdensville, Mooresville, Salisbury, Raleigh, and Gastonia, North Carolina.[56]

In the upper Piedmont the series of strikes almost stopped in 1920.  At Rock Hill and Carhart, South Carolina, the union closed two mills in April, on the grounds of discrimination and the refusal of the company to permit grievances to be carried higher than the superintendent.  After a week's idleness the company began evictions and arrested pickets with trespass warrants.  The dispute reached a climax, the local's business agent said, "in the killing of a fine brave man who had violated his obligations to the union"[57]—apparently a strikebreaker.  Settlements were finally reached, the one signed early in 1921 providing for re-

[55] Proc., ibid., 1919, p. 59; Daily News, Greensboro, Sept. 30; Observer, Charlotte, Aug. 13; News and Observer, Raleigh, Aug. 13, Sept. 15-18, 1919; Daily News Record, New York, Aug. 14, Sept. 13, 19, 1919.
[56] Proc., ibid., 1919, pp. 86, 87; Daily News Record, April 11, Sept. 15, Oct. 28, 30, Nov. 1, Dec. 2, 1919; Southern Textile Bulletin Nov. 20, 1919, p. 14.
[57] Proc., ibid., 1920, p. 133.

instatement of all persons concerned.[58] A dispute at Landis, North Carolina, in the same year, was unconnected with union issues.[59]

The breathless organizing and the rapid-fire strikes in North Carolina kept up for only six or seven months. Late in 1919 the movement had begun to slow, and although the union kept a string of organizers busy in the mills through most of 1920, it failed to hold its membership. Only 30 new locals were formed in the whole South in the twelve months after September, 1919. In the region below North Carolina even the patchy unionism of 1913-1918 faded away. When the depression set in in earnest in 1921, it found the union movement concentrated in a belt of mills in Piedmont North Carolina; outside them most of the locals were reduced to a skeleton membership and many had disappeared. Finally, what strength was left in the North Carolina unions consumed itself in a three months' strike in the summer of 1921. When the A. F. of L. launched an ambitious reorganizing campaign a few months after the strike, it met no response. Propaganda carried no appeal to a population working short time, hanging on in villages where the mills had been shut for weeks or months, and badly in need of what wages the mills would offer. By the end of the year hardly a single healthy union remained in the Southern mills.

Columbus, the last city in the lower South in which the union held together at all, steadily lost its membership. In 1920 the best efforts of the U. T. W. officials failed to pro-

[58] *Proc., ibid.,* pp. 177-78; ibid., 1921, p. 114; *Textile Worker,* Aug., 1920, p. 280.

[59] *Observer,* Charlotte, July 8-11, 1920; *Southern Textile Bulletin,* July 15, 1920.

duce a revival. In 1921, when wage cuts and short-time operation led something over a thousand operatives in one mill to strike, no more success in signing members had been had and the workers after three months gave in on the employers' terms.[60]

In North Carolina, where many of the unions were still intact, the movement pushed itself slowly to destruction. From late 1920 on through the spring of 1921 the mills were steadily reducing wages. By May the cuts ranged between thirty and fifty per cent in a full day's earnings, and many of the mills were finding it difficult to provide work for three or four days in the week. When the cuts began, the business agents of the Carolina locals asked the U. T. W. officials for endorsement of a strike. Golden, with his treasury low from the long Northern strikes of 1920, advised against it. The Southern organizers were told to "explain to the members why they should remain at work."[61] But with new reductions the Southerners became insistent. They may have believed that a determined stand would bring back some of the lost wages; also their business agents were trying to overcome the waning interest of their members who argued, "if the union won't fight, why pay dues?"[62] The U. T. W. had a direct interest in organizing resistance to

[60] *Proc., ibid.*, 1920, p. 176; *Enquirer-Sun*, Columbus, Nov. 12, 1920-March 31, April 3, 1921; *Ledger*, Columbus, March 30, April 6, 1921; *Observer*, Charlotte, May 3, 1921.

[61] *Proc., ibid.*, 1921, p. 113.

[62] In February, one of the Southern business agents in urging strike endorsement at a union council, stated that if he failed to gain the International's consent for a strike his local would have to lapse about five hundred members. President Golden argued that inasmuch as the union wanted to see the cotton workers organized, "he did not care if the whole membership stopped paying their dues, that the International would not give endorsement of a strike when we knew we were defeated before we began." (*Ibid.*)

the Southern wage reductions. The cut in New England had been only 22½ per cent; if 40 per cent were allowed to stand in the South, the pressure on the New England rate would be greater. But the union's membership was dropping away by thousands, its own funds were small, and it could expect little assistance from the trade union world. In this dilemma it compromised. It agreed with the Southern leaders, and subsequently with a conference of representatives of forty local unions in the Carolina mills that the U. T. W. would conduct a strike, but that the right to the constitutional strike benefit would be waived, and that the U. T. W. would give only such assistance as its funds would permit.[63]    On this basis plans went ahead.

In the illness of President Golden, the union's vice-president, T. F. McMahon, was sent into the section. He called the strike finally on June 1. About 9,000 workers in mills belonging for the most part to three large companies, but including a number of independents, and strung through Rock Hill, Huntersville, Charlotte, Concord, and Kannapolis, came out. It did not take long for the shortage of funds to make itself felt. The locals were supplying through

[63] The conference consisted of two delegates from each union, and was held at Concord, April 30. The officers said after the strike that they explained that the U. T. W. "was not in a position to pay that amount of strike pay, but they would do all that was in their power to help them" and warned of the sacrifices that a strike would bring. "The vote was unanimous to carry out the policy of the International Union." The officers then "visited every local union and mass meetings were called to explain to them the policy of the International Union; in every instance the vote was unanimous to follow out the policy . . ." (*ibid.*, pp. 113, 114). "The Southerners came there (to New York) and told us their story, of how they were being imposed upon by reduction after reduction, and appealed to us to let them go on. They were told frankly that the International did not have the money to finance a big fight under these conditions. . . . They waived all claim to it. All they asked us was that we send all we could to them, and they would spend it to the best advantage." (Delegate Tobias Hall, *ibid.*, p. 590.) *Cf. Observer*, Charlotte, May 3, June 2, 1921.

commissaries about 8,000 workers and their dependents. Contributions from the union members at work outside the strike zone were small; the International Union, though it professed afterward to have given all it had or could collect, sent down only a few thousand dollars, and the locals and their leaders went heavily into debt. Meanwhile, most of the mills struck had no inclination to resume operations; some of them were not sorry for an excuse to stand idle; they took no active steps to end the strike but simply waited until the union should crumble and the operatives offer themselves for work.

When the plight of the strikers had had time to sink in, a bold propaganda campaign, managed by a Charlotte trade journal, exploited to the full the union's weakness in endorsing the strike. A series of advertisements in Charlotte dailies, backed by editorial diatribes in the *Southern Textile Bulletin,* presented the anti-U. T. W. arguments. It was contended, first, that living costs in the vicinity of Charlotte had fallen as much as or more than the wage of the mill workers, and therefore the protest against the wage reduction was unreasonable; and second, that the union had used the Southern workers with bad faith. Said the Charlotte editor: "If you [President McMahon] cannot give this relief [the constitutional strike benefit of six dollars per week for the 8,000 operatives] you knew when you called the strike that you would not be able to give it, and you deceived and betrayed the mill operatives of this section"; and again: "If the union has no funds, what has become of the dues that have been paid in during these months and years that the Textile workers have belonged to it?" The editor claimed that "the strike was defeated by an aroused public sentiment which came as a result of a campaign of publicity conducted by the *Southern Textile Bulletin* and its editor."[64]

[64] *Southern Textile Bulletin,* Aug. 25, 1921, p. 18.

The collapse came in the last two weeks of August. Although toward the end of the dispute it was stated that "both sides agree that there has been virtually no tendency towards violence, and relatively speaking, good spirit prevailed,"[65] when the mills began to reopen, returning workers at Concord were roughly treated. National Guardsmen came in to preserve order there and at Kannapolis while the mills started. In most of the towns work was resumed on terms that left no shred of success for the union. The wage scale in effect June 1 was continued; in only one or two instances was provision made for future meetings with committees; and no guarantee of complete reëmployment was obtained. Many leaders were refused places, and some weeks after the strikes were officially over hundreds of strikers were still without work.

In extent, in number of workers involved, in public notice, and in the heat to which passion was aroused this strike was by far the most serious that had occurred thus far in the Southern mills. It demonstrated that collective action was possible to the Southern operatives, even under adverse conditions. What was more important in the subsequent history of unionism in the section, it left behind a widespread belief that the U. T. W. leaders had in one form or another used trickery.

The hosiery and cotton mills of East Tennessee have been separated so effectually from the industry on the other side of the mountain chain that, so far as unionism is concerned, events in one region have had little influence in the other. The exception is the position of leadership in the Southern movement held by the local in Knoxville, whose 1,200 members, between 1912 and 1921 were offered no resistance by their employer, and which in consequence was

[65] *Daily News*, Greensboro, Aug. 14, 1921.

able to contribute organizers and funds to the agitation in the Piedmont. In Tennessee the union has had an advantage in the diversified industry of the region and in unusually loyal aid of the unions of metal workers and others. With the constant help of the Knoxville local, the U. T. W. kept up an irregular movement from 1912 until the depression, and since then organization has reappeared perhaps with more strength than in the Carolinas.

The agitation here as elsewhere in the South has not resulted, however, in continuous organization, but in successive disputes. The first was a brief and unsuccessful strike of some 600 hosiery mill workers at Lenoir City, in 1915, over discharges held to be discriminatory.[66] Two years later at Chattanooga, the textile workers shared in a general unionizing movement. In May the mill people caught the fire from recently organized municipal workers and when discharges of union operatives began, the forces in eight or nine mills ceased work. The demand was union recognition. U. T. W. agents and local labor leaders took charge. The companies argued that war production required immediate return to work, and refused to treat with the union. A network of injunctions, the comic boastfulness of a Federal mediator, petty violence on the part of the strikers, the sending in of a knot of State troopers, and the easy descent of a U. T. W. organizer into a discreditable situation, made the dispute lively and at the same time "one of the most bitterly contested strikes the South ever had." When the workers had been out two months, mediation by a Chattanooga editor secured the reinstatement of all but a handful, though a hundred of the workers who went back earlier had been required to surrender their union cards.[67] Although the union

[66] Proc., ibid., 1915, p .46.
[67] Proc., ibid., 1917, pp. 45, 56, 57; Daily Times, Chattanooga, May 18-Aug. 2, 1917.

failed to win recognition, it had a large membership when the strike was over and boasted of several "virtually closed union shops."[68]   But the locals could not have been strong early in 1919.   When on February 3 the walkout on the eight-hour issue was called, only a few score of workers left the Chattanooga mills, in spite of much exhortation before the day set.   The employers countered the move of the few who left by operating on a six-and-one-half-hours' schedule until the disturbance had quieted down.[69]

Late in 1919 a four weeks' lockout in Nashville was settled with some concessions to unionist sentiment.[70]

With the depression in 1921 the union lost its favorable position in Knoxville.   The operatives collectively accepted a first cut in wages of 22½ per cent when a similar reduction was made in New England.   Two months afterwards, when the employer offered a resumption of full-time operation coupled with a second cut of 22½ per cent, the union refused the terms and stayed out for eleven weeks.   The long strike weakened the operatives' enthusiasm, and when the mill reopened the union dwindled away.   In 1923 an organizer who visited the city was opposed by the company and failed to reëstablish the local.[71]

Some agitation continued, however, without the help from Knoxville.   At Chattanooga, in the summer of 1923, a local which scored a success in one mill with a two days' strike for wage advances and changed conditions, a few weeks later met stronger opposition from the management. Grievances about discharges and an obstinate foreman were

[68] *Proc., ibid.,* p. 61.

[69] *Chronicle,* Augusta, Ga., Feb. 4; *Daily Times,* Chattanooga, Feb. 2-9; *Observer,* Charlotte, Feb. 4, 1919.

[70] *Proc., ibid.,* 1919, p. 60; *Daily News Record,* New York, Sept. 9, 30, 1919.

[71] *Proc. ibid.,* 1921, p. 115; 1922, p. 571; 1923, p. 400; *Observer,* Charlotte, May 2, 3, 1921.

allowed to develop into a strike of boarders. Material was sent to a branch mill at Bristol, but girl boarders there went out also. The Bristol strikers were replaced and at Chattanooga after two months the men gave in, surrendering their organization.[72] Early in the next year when mills at South Pittsburg and Whitwell announced a 15 per cent reduction in wages for certain of their workers, the unorganized operatives walked out to resist the changes. Union representatives were sent in, and, with aid from local unions of molders and mounters, the workers were supported for sixteen weeks, when mediation by outside trade unionists and business men induced the mills to resume without the wage cuts and with no discrimination against union workers.[73]

For years after the South Pittsburg strike a tiny local there was the only body of organized workers in the region.

Back in the Piedmont the U. T. W.'s movement was very weak for nearly ten years after the close of the 1921 strike. Until 1926 the proportion of depressed mills was large enough to make a job in a mill that was running well too valuable to be risked. The Northern union has since 1922 been hampered by the thinning of its ranks consequent upon the New England depression, and until recently had difficulty in keeping even one organizer in the Southern field. But it is doubtful if more prosperity and a better-off union in the North would have made it possible for a strong organization to have appeared in the South in these years. Periodically union campaigns were launched in the mills,

[72] *Proc., ibid.,* 1924, pp. 490, 604, 605; Matthew J. Robinson, interview, Chattanooga, June 12, 1924; *Daily Times,* Chattanooga, Sept. 6, 1923; *Daily News Record,* Sept. 7, 1923; *Textile Worker,* Sept., 1923, p. 334.

[73] *Proc., ibid.,* 1924, p. 490; *Textile Worker,* Aug., 1924, p. 270; Miss Anna Neary, interview, Baltimore, Md., Dec. 20, 1925; *Daily News Record,* New York, July 23, 1924.

sometimes with the help of the A. F. of L., and all were withdrawn through failure both to sign members and to settle disputes as to leadership and methods. But some agitation was kept up. In 1922 and 1923 the union reorganized in ten or a dozen Carolina towns tiny locals of "fire-tested" unionists—not more than a few hundred altogether. These operatives revived the old council of the Charlotte area locals, as the Joint Council of the Textile Workers of the Two Carolinas, and sent delegates with some regularity to its monthly meetings. The Council concerned itself mostly with plans for new campaigns, with hopeful reports of the reissue of an occasional old charter, and with censure upon the State legislatures. The movement was helped between 1922 and 1925 by the propaganda issuing from J. F. Barrett's "Charlotte Herald," which abused the employers after the manner of the Lancashire chartist weeklies of the 'forties. It was probably directly responsible for the weak strikes in Charlotte in 1922 and 1923—the last a three days "orderly protest strike" of a few workers at one mill brought on by discrimination against the operative responsible for an article critical of welfare work which appeared in the *Herald*.[74] A few more disputes occurred: at Rocky Mount late in 1922, at Greensboro in 1925, and at Lexington in 1926.[75] The last two were spontaneous strikes, the first a brief contest by card room hands against new shop requirements, that ended with cancellation of eviction orders, and an adjustment of the grievance; and the second a week's walkout of weavers in one mill against wage cuts.

If the U. T. W.'s own activity was slight, it began to

[74] *Textile Worker,* Oct., 1922, p. 403; Nov., pp. 470, 472; *ibid.,* Sept., 1923, p. 336; *Observer,* Charlotte, Aug. 18, 25; *Times,* Raleigh, Aug. 20; *Times,* Concord, Aug. 23; *Southern Textile Bulletin,* Aug. 30; *Daily News Record,* New York, Aug. 15, 27, 1923.

[75] *Textile Worker,* Nov., 1922, pp. 470, 471; Oct., 1926, p. 403; *Daily News,* Greensboro, Aug. 31-Sept. 5, 1925.

have gratuitous aid in 1925 from another source. In 1924 mills making full-fashioned hosiery began establishing themselves in the South. The industry in its Philadelphia center has long been held closely organized by the American Federation of Full-Fashioned Hosiery Workers. That union, in order to meet the spread of its mills to low-wage cities elsewhere, has had to develop progressive policies and accumulate substantial reserves. It has a membership of ten or twelve thousand operatives, many of them highly skilled and drawing wages treble or quadruple those of other textile workers. The new Southern shops, paying wages from 50 to 60 per cent below the Philadelphia scale, at once drew the union's fire.[76] An organizer has been kept in the region most of the time since the summer of 1925, carrying forward a campaign to unionize the shops and force an approximation of the Northern standards. The union has put out feelers in many Southern shops and has conducted strikes in two or three.[77] At Durham, knitters in one plant struck twice in 1925; the first time successfully against being required to train non-union apprentices; and the second time, a few weeks later, unsuccessfully for a rise in wages and against discrimination. Union agitation continued in the city and seamless boarders went out twice in 1927, to return after each strike without concessions.

Meanwhile at Burlington, discrimination at a small plant and an attempt to require anti-union contracts, brought out a handful of union knitters, whom the employer replaced with a large staff of unskilled operatives working under supervision from one or two trained men. In these disputes the union lost, but the favorable position in which skill places the

[76] William Smith, secretary, A. F. F. F. H. W., interview, Philadelphia, Dec. 16, 1927.
[77] The Hosiery Worker, May 16-Aug. 1, 1927.

knitters makes it probable that the attempt to organize will continue. Strong pressure can be placed upon employers. Most of the plants are small and without great capital resources; their overhead expenses require steady production if they are to show a profit. The union, on the other hand, is able to pay a high strike benefit indefinitely; at Durham it continued payment to some of its members for almost a year. Its control of the majority of the Northern knitters and its ability to tempt trained men in the South with offers of well-paid Northern jobs, gives it leverage in preventing mills from getting skilled knitters as strikebreakers. Yet the costliness and delicacy of the machines makes it doubtful policy for an employer to use untrained help. Also, the union finds its organizing work made easier by the fact that only a few of the plants have adopted company housing. These advantages the Federation has exploited with a constant effort to embarrass as many non-union mills as it could reach.[78]  But against the union's chances of success must be counted the scattered situation of the shops, the ease with which the learners can be secured, and the concentration of opposition to the union from the surrounding textile industry, which sees in the hosiery union an entering wedge for cotton mill organization. The Federation in its Southern activity has coöperated with the U. T. W. to which it as a union belongs. It is conscious of the possibility that the skill of its members will enable it to reproduce in the South the position of the old mulespinners in New England, who are proud that for

[78] "The manufacturer (in the Southern shops) is becoming nothing more than a teacher of knitters, with an enormous loss through large labor turnover, and with low production, depreciation of machinery, a ridiculously high percentage of waste and bad work, and the expense of teaching knitters who want to work elsewhere." (*Hosiery Worker,* Oct. 1, 1927.) *Cf. Proc.,* A. F. F. F. H. W., 1927, pp. 29-32.

many years they "fought the battle of all the textile workers alone."[79]

In the only important strike which occurred in the Piedmont between 1921 and 1929, the hosiery union played a leading part.  In the summer of 1927, entirely unorganized workers at Henderson, remembering the half-promise after a brief walkout three years earlier to restore, when conditions should permit, part of a cut accepted then, petitioned in one mill for the advance in wages, and for the doing away with a new and irksome gate rule.  The operatives left the mill in a pique when it was rumored that the petition had not been treated with respect.  Pickets promptly carried out the forces in two more mills, and reduced the number in a fourth, until eight or nine hundred workers were out.  The employers had difficulty in organizing a force of deputies, and when the strikers threatened to prevent maintenance men from entering, the plants telephoned for State troops.  Military companies came in, but found no disorder and were withdrawn after two days.  A squad of North Carolina labor men went to the town and the Hosiery Federation's organizer, coöperating with the local leaders, took charge.  The hosiery union voted and collected relief money and advised the strikers to remain out for the 12½ per cent.  A difference in policy between the U. T. W. and the hosiery union prevented the U. T. W.'s taking part in the strike, and when five or six hundred prospective members were signed (initiation fees were not collected) the U. T. W. made no effort to keep a local in the town.  It argued the wisdom of avoiding blame for the inevitable defeat of unorganized workers.  After a month of idleness, during which the employers showed no disposition to yield, the strike was ended by the balancing of the operatives' feeling of loyalty

[79] *Proc.*, International Spinners Union, 1917, p. 6.

to fifteen families which the mill ordered evicted against the desire to prolong the stand for the wage increase.   In the absence of the organizer, the workers voted to return to the mills unconditionally.   Work was resumed on Labor Day.[80]

[80] *Hosiery Worker,* Sept. 1, 1927; *Southern Textile Bulletin,* Sept. 8; *Southern Textile Bulletin, Home Edition,* Aug. 25, Sept. 15, Sept. 22; *Survey,* Nov. 15; *New Masses,* Dec.; *Locomotive Engineer's Journal,* Dec.; *Daily News,* Greensboro, Aug. 11-Sept. 12; *News and Observer,* Raleigh, Aug. 11-27; *Observer,* Charlotte, Aug. 11-Sept. 10.

# CHAPTER III

## RECENT ACTIVITY

WHILE it was the entry of the skilled craft of hosiery knitters and the agitation conducted among them by the Philadelphia knitters' union that prepared the way for a turn of the union tide in the Southern cotton mills, it was the Henderson strike which really brought up again the possibility of general organization in the mills. The State Federation of Labor had been directly interested in the dispute, and, in coöperation with the State labor officials, the Hosiery Union began to spread its activity over a larger field. The first step was the formation, late in 1927, of the Piedmont Organizing Council. This body began a series of monthly meetings of delegates and members of local unions from a dozen or more towns in Central Carolina, bringing into some meetings more than a score of different crafts.[1] It shifted its meetings through most of the industrial cities of North Carolina, and in each brought together enthusiastic and sizable groups. The mainspring behind it was the energy of the representative of the Hosiery Workers, Alfred Hoffman, who, in turn, drew on his training at Brookwood Labor College in New York. Hoffman had sincere support from the established union officials and the central labor unions, and through them two or three local labor papers were revivified. The Piedmont Organizing Council, besides its local propaganda, invited the A. F. of L. to give help with general organizing work in the South, encouraged a union drive in the

[1] Among the trades represented at a typical meeting when the movement was well under way were: marble setters, plasterers, lathers, railway trainmen, meat cutters, railway clerks, carpenters, bricklayers, machinists, hosiery workers, printers, pressmen, plumbers, molders tobacco workers painters, stone masons, garment workers, hod-carriers, stage employees, book-binders, and blacksmiths (*Union Herald,* Raleigh, N. C., May 31, 1928).

tobacco factories of Durham and Winston-Salem, and kept before the craft unionists the desirability of organization in the textile mills.

In the spring of 1928 membership in many of the craft unions within the area began to grow. The success of the North Carolina council led to the formation of similar bodies in Virginia and South Carolina, with like propaganda. These bodies, through the influence of the State federations of labor, were partly responsible for renewed plans for a widespread Southern campaign. At the end of October, 1928, delegates from six State federations met at Chattanooga to discuss such a campaign. Though coal unionism was the main topic, the delegates from Georgia and North Carolina talked about conditions in the cotton mills, and the low wages of mill girls in Tennessee were given attention also. This meeting was followed by a "caucus" of Southern delegates at the New Orleans convention of the American Federation of Labor, where a drive for organization, with the various unions working together, was mapped out.

Thus, by the beginning of 1929, the local craft unions in the mill regions were gathering strength, the State federations and the labor press were on tip-toes for further expansion, and the A. F. of L. was committed to a big Southern campaign.

In the meantime a gradual change had come over the United Textile Workers. In the old years of rising standards in the Northern industry, artificially prolonged by the war into 1920, the union had been too busy with a ceaseless round of strikes to consider anything beyond relief and battle for victory. After the agonized fights against declining wages and lengthening hours in 1921 and 1922, few Northern textile locals were in a condition to do more than grimly hold what they had, and except for occasional big strikes, such as those at Passaic and New Bedford, the union was not heavily involved in disputes. Dwindling membership and a slim treasury did not increase combativeness. In these circumstances, the U. T. W. was prepared for acceptance of the A. F. of L.'s new policy of coöperativeness. This was the more true since the union had within its own ranks, after 1924, the example of the free coöperation of union and management in the Naumkeag Steam Cotton Mills at Salem, Massachusetts; since the affiliated union of Hosiery Workers was trying for a collective agreement with its employers; and since some "intellectual" influence from the old Amalgamated Textile Workers had survived to assist the U. T. W. By 1927 or 1928 the United Textile Workers had adopted as a settled policy union assistance to management in matters of mill operation, and, as a concomitant, it was emphasizing the use of strikes only as a "last resort." These doctrines had been implicit all along in the union's "conservative" tendency, but by 1929 they had been given definite form and could be relied upon to appear in any new expansion of the organization. "Militancy" was also reduced by a constitutional rule adopted some years earlier, excluding from endorsement and official support, except in unusual circumstances, strikes which occurred in places where the workers had not been well organized for at least six months. Long experience of bearing the burden of defeat in strikes which were despairing from the beginning had taught caution.

That the new policy is a more acceptable one to mill management and to middle-class opinion in the South than the old readiness to fight does not need argument; its advantage to Southern mill workers, which is disputed in some quarters, is at present being tested.

With Southern trade unionism in general prepared for a new advance, and the United Textile Workers' ideology altered to one apt to make Southern entry easier, a spread into the South awaited only a favoring economic period and open exhibit of discontent by Southern operatives.

Both these latter came in the spring of 1929. Southern mills had for nearly a decade monopolized what prosperity the cotton industry could show, and though they suffered from overproduction, and often operated irregularly, as a whole 1929 found them not depressed. The impetus to economy was nevertheless strong. New England mills had recently been winning back a thin margin of profit by doubling machinery, particularly by installing more scientific systems of loom operation, and the same process was beginning to be widespread in the South. An old industrial population, accustomed to discipline, conscious of the dangerous position of the mills in which it worked, and feebly organized, protested little against the new methods which scientific managers introduced, particularly when some consultation of the operatives was had, and the union was able to propagandize for wage increases that should accompany increases of machines per man. In the South, however, efficiency systems were usually installed after perfunctory exhortation of the employees as to loyalty, often by Northern experts who were not sufficiently tender of the self-respect of the Southern operatives; in some cases there were no wage advances, or there were even reductions. The result was an undercurrent of dissatisfaction with the "stretch-out," which drew about it the ever-present discontent with long hours and low wages—a combination that led to explosion.

The spade-work of the Piedmont Organizing Council, the announced readiness of the A. F. of L. to give assistance, the new language of the U. T. W., relative prosperity, and the immediate grievance of the stretch-out in scores of mills, were the ingredients out of which the present and biggest union advance in the South was made.

In spite of all this heightened agitation, in 1928 and early 1929 little impression seemed to have been made on the textile operatives. The U. T. W. was doing little more than it had in any year since 1921 to found locals in the South; indeed no representative of its own was regularly in the region while the Piedmont Organizing Council was being perfected. But that the agitation had been seeping down among the mill workers is abundantly shown by the sudden flowering of organized unrest in the spring of 1929. In a period of a few weeks in March and April, strikes broke out in four widely separated districts: in Eastern Tennessee, at Elizabethton; in Piedmont South Carolina; in the North Carolina mountains, at Marion; and in the heart of the upper Piedmont, at Gastonia. In none of these places, it is true, had any important direct organizing work been carried on just before the strikes, and the immediate causes of the strikes were general grievances rather than a desire for organization. When the strikes occurred the people, in most of the towns affected, accepted whatever sort of union leadership offered itself most promptly, showing that they had no clear notion of the union movement as a whole; but the noisier preachment of unionism in the last couple of years must certainly have influenced the revolt.

The first strike, that at Elizabethton, though it had been preceded by some union talk, had at first the character of one of the old "turn-outs" of the New England mill girls in the 'forties. East Tennessee had had a good many visits from union organizers and three or four strikes between 1923 and 1926, and the United Textile Workers had actually had a charter at Elizabethton for some time in 1927-28. A brief strike had occurred in January, 1929. But the big strike began without any union impetus. The town was a mountain place which had slumbered all its history until two great German rayon mills were built there, only two or three years before the strike. The call for help was insistent, and the hill people had crowded into inadequate housing at high rents, or were coming long distances by hired motor-cars to their work each day. Real estate owners were counting the increments to the value of their valley strips as the population grew. The quick change to industrial occupation, under difficult conditions and at low wages, spread discontent.

When the foreman of a roomful of girls made an unpopular choice for promotion, the girls supported their leader, and 150 of them walked out. In two days the whole mill was on strike, local building tradesmen were forming a textile union, and demands for a 25 per cent wage increase and union recognition had been made. The Tennessee State Federation of Labor took charge for a few days, and a week after the strike had begun turned it over to Alfred Hoffman and Miss Matilda Lindsay of the Women's Trade Union League. Since the strike had occurred without the six months of prior organization that the U. T. W.'s rule required for endorsement, funds had to be found in the union by appeal.

When the strike was at its height, both plants were closed and nearly 5,000 people were out. Picketing, begun a week after the strike started, brought two companies of National Guardsmen, for constitutional reasons spoken of as "State police," and injunctions were issued. Partly through the intervention of a United States Commissioner of Conciliation, the strike was settled after eleven days under agreed terms providing for return of the workers under the open shop plan with no discrimination against the union. Men's wages in the two plants were to be equalized, and women's wages were to be raised about 20 per cent; grievances were to be settled by conferences of employe committees with plant officials; troops and injunctions were to be withdrawn.[2]

During the strike the union organizers had signed several hundred members, and to the townspeople it appeared that the union was to be permanent, and expectations of the town's growth were accordingly lowered. In this situation the business men became embattled. A party of them in several automobiles seized organizers Hoffman and McGrady at their hotel and carried them at night, one across the State line into North Carolina and the other into West Virginia. Before they were put down the organizers were warned against returning to Elizabethton. The two organizers got in touch with the A. F. of L. headquarters, and President William Green accompanied them back to the strike scene. Thereafter the union organizers walked about in company with an armed guard of Tennessee mountaineers.

The excitement of the kidnapping and resentment against the discharge of a number of unionists, brought on a "wild cat strike," beginning the middle of April. The first strike had been relatively peaceful; this time a good deal more violence appeared on both sides. Four thousand people were out the first day, and troops poured in to the number of three companies. Parades, picketing on the open road miles away from the plant, machine guns on the mill roof, motor-cycle squads, gas bombs, dynamiting of water mains, and arrests were in evidence for more than a month. This time, however, the mills were able gradually to recruit working forces, and, when a settlement was made through conciliation and conferences, the mills were by no means under such pressure as in the first case. It was arranged that the company would employ a personnel manager acceptable to the union, that

[2] *Journal,* Knoxville, Tenn., March 3, 1929.

the company would continue to treat with committees, and that all except a few "undesirables" would be reëmployed. Again a promise of no discrimination was given.[3]

By this time the union is said to have had a membership of several thousand, but the plants had organized a company union, against which the U. T. W. has since fought a losing battle. The town has continued to have disturbances, and once or twice Federal conciliators have been sent down again.

In March, 1930, the trade union element, finding its position weak, attempted to draw support to itself by a third and very incomplete strike. Injunctions and deputy sheriffs again suppressed vigorous picketing, and within a week the strike collapsed. Sporadic violence and dynamiting have continued.

Two things should be remarked of the strikers in Elizabethton. Their elemental sense of justice showed itself in active individual resentment of compulsions brought in on the side of the management, and at the same time in their mass meetings they exhibited reasonableness and mature self-respect.

East of the mountains, in the principal center of the old movement of 1919-21, a startling development was beginning at the time of the Elizabethton strike. In 1928 the Communist Party in the United States had, upon orders from the Third Internationale, abandoned its former policy of boring from within, and had determined to establish trade unions of its own. In accordance with this policy, the Communists had used the wreck of the Passaic and New Bedford strikes to form a National Textile Workers Union. This organization delegated Fred Beal to try to spread unionism into the Southern field.

[3] *Ibid.*, May 26.

Beal was in and out of Gastonia for some months early in 1929, and by April of that year he had formed a small local of the Communist union. On April 2, several members of this local were discharged from the Loray Mill, and within two days about 2,000 workers from the mill had come out, and many are said to have joined the National Textile Workers Union.

As a protest, the strike proper lasted a little over two weeks, though it was not until the end of May that the mill was in its old pace of operation. The demands of the Communists were for a five-day, forty-hour week, a twenty-dollar minimum wage, better housing, cheaper rents, and union recognition. None of these demands were granted, though the mill did resume operation at a fifty-hour week, in agreement with many other mills in the section.

It is not the strictly economic phase of the strike which is of most interest. The most arresting element in the whole disturbance is the ready acceptance by large numbers of the Gastonia workers of the Communist leadership. Fred Beal and a group of other Communist organizers from the North, preached from the first the whole Communist doctrine— revolution, racial equality, syndicalist operation of the mill, and internationalism. The Gastonia mill people can hardly have had a clear understanding of the oratory to which they listened, but it is significant of their sense of injustice done them that they entered enthusiastically into the program of the leaders. As in the I. W. W. strike in Greenville in 1913, Gastonia and the South awoke with a start. Gastonia as a town is to an unusual degree dependent upon the cotton manufacturing industry. Its commercial elements were, therefore, the more aghast at the Communist explosion. From the first they determined to remove the Communist group by fair means or foul. The violence which followed was largely on their side.

In the second day of the strike, an occasion for bringing in eight companies of National Guardsmen was found in a scuffle incident to the stretching of a rope outside the mill. The number of soldiers was gradually reduced during the first three weeks, and deputy sheriffs to the number of forty remained in their place. The presence of the last of the troops was not sufficient to prevent demolition of the strikers' commissary and headquarters by what may be called the "civic element."

Except for minor clashes during parades which the Communists organized in violation of a local ordinance, little further violence occurred until long after the strike had become hopeless. About fifty families had, however, been evicted from the company's houses, and the desperation of these people, living in a tent colony put up by the Communist organization, led to the major tragedy of the strike. A renewed attempt at picketing one afternoon early in June was violently repulsed, and the strikers retreated to their settlement.

For some time, the leaders of the strike had kept up an armed guard at their new headquarters. The city police were summoned, it is said, to the tent colony to settle an internal row at the headquarters. When they arrived at the building, the Communists on guard interpreted their appearance as a new raid, and resisted. In the firing which followed, the Gastonia chief of police, Aderholt, was killed outright and one of his deputies was wounded. The affray then became a raid proper, and was followed by a reign of violence for several days, during which Communists and union sympathizers were persecuted.

After this occurrence, the issue changed from an industrial one to the question how Gastonia could rid itself in the quickest way of the Communists. There followed a lull, with most of the leaders in jail for the murder of Aderholt. New leaders who came down were in one case treated to a night ride and a flogging. Some days later, September 13, a truck load of union members coming to Gastonia from Bessemer City was forced by Gastonia citizens to turn back, and was pursued by several automobiles. A few miles from Gastonia the truck was forcibly stopped, and Ella May Wiggins, one of those in the truck, was killed by a bullet,— place of origin unknown.

This incident closed the strike. The legal prosecutions claim attention. Throughout the trials, convictions for violence on the part of the strikers were uniformly had, and in no case was anyone accused of injury to a striker found guilty. The grand jury investigation of the first raid on the commissary failed to find enough evidence to indict anybody. In the Aderholt case, tried in Charlotte, on the ground that a fair trial could not be had in Gaston County, the original process against sixteen men and women strikers ended in a mistrial. A month later, seven of these strikers were tried again, the charge now being reduced from first to second degree murder. In the trial the prosecuting attorney was allowed wide latitude in that he was permitted to show the beliefs of the Communists, particularly as to the use of force as an instrument in social change. The testimony of one defense witness was stricken out because of avowed atheism. The seven men tried were convicted and sentenced to terms of imprisonment varying from five to twenty years; the one local man was given the shortest sentence. The defense appealed, and the men were allowed bail.

The trial of four members of the band which had kidnapped three of the Communist leaders ended in acquittal, with the jury apparently accepting the defense theory that the kidnapping and beating had been a Communist-organized publicity "stunt."

The trial for the murder of Ella May Wiggins, like that of Aderholt, went through two stages. The grand jury, the same which had indicted the sixteen men in the Aderholt shooting, refused to indict the nine men ordered held by the coroner's jury for the death of Mrs. Wiggins. The Governor of the State sent in a committing magistrate, who, after hearings, bound over fourteen men for trial. When the case came up, the prosecution built up what appeared to be an excellent case against five Loray Mill employees. One man was identified by several people who had been in the truck as the firer of the fatal shot. The defense, however, presented alibis which convinced the jury, and the verdict was acquittal.

As to the whole Gastonia episode, it may be said that the Communists at first had expectations of establishing a genuine Communist trade union. These expectations were based on the prompt acceptance by the Gastonia strikers of the Communist leadership, and the formation of small local unions elsewhere nearby—at Charlotte, Lexington, Bessemer City, Pineville, and Leaksville, among others. Two conventions of delegates from these locals were held in the region. This trade union side of the program, which was sincere with the leaders, was what appealed most to the Southern operatives. The fervor of the leaders in advocating the policy of revolutionary class-consciousness met little bewilderment. It is noteworthy, however, that in Gastonia, at any rate, attempts to destroy the agitation by discrediting the Communists' advocacy of racial equality had no success.

The Gastonia strike largely destroyed the trade union side of the Communist agitation. Since then, Communist agents have appeared from time to time all through the Southern mill region, district headquarters have been kept open, and Communists, some from the South, have been arrested at Winston-Salem, Atlanta, Chattanooga, Lumberton, North Carolina, and elsewhere. The failure to recruit any membership since the Gastonia strike, at a time when their much-abused rival, the U. T. W., has been growing rapidly, would indicate, however, the practical elimination of the National Textile Workers Union from the South. Meantime the stir at Elizabethton and Gastonia was influencing even the more isolated mills. At one of these, the Marion Manufacturing Company, at Marion, North Carolina, dissatisfied operatives had clubbed together to raise enough money to send one of their number over to Elizabethton to ask for a visit from an organizer. Help could not be had in Elizabethton, but from Asheville trade unionists came in. Early in July, the Marion local union, which by then is said to have included over half of the mill operatives, petitioned the management for a reduction of the maximum working day from 12 hours and 20 minutes to 10 hours, and for reinstatement of a number of discharged unionists.

Failing to obtain satisfaction, the union committee called a strike on July 11, when all of the 650 employees left the mill. This strike lasted for nine weeks, and for a time was enlarged by a strike and lockout of the 1,000 employes of the Clinchfield Mills nearby.

The distinctive characteristic of this strike was its leadership. Though the local union had called forth leaders of its own, these men were directed by the outside organizers and labor sympathizers who came into the situation. At the time of the strike, the United Textile Workers was deeply involved at Elizabethton, and sent no one directly representing it to Marion. The breach was filled by Alfred Hoffman and two or three associates connected with the Brookwood Labor College in New York. These men shared the coolness toward the A. F. of L. shown by the Conference for Progressive Labor Action. They disagreed with the coöperative policy being urged by the U. T. W., and carried into Marion a philosophical militancy. The violence which occurred in this strike and in the succeeding one was probably due in some degree to their desire to hit back at oppression of the workers. Evictions were met with physical resistance, impassable mass picket lines were occasionally used, and with rough handling of mill officials. A month after the strike began, these methods brought several companies of troops to the town.

Settlement of the strike came in two stages. The Clinchfield Mills were able to reopen in an orderly fashion by promising reinstatement and by permitting the union to check the workers as they returned. The Marion Mill, after conferences with a representative of Governor Gardner, and other intervention, settled on a basis of a temporary fifty-five hour schedule, maintenance of the existing hourly and piece rates, with no discrimination against employes on the ground of union membership. In the ensuing weeks the union found itself unable to obtain reëmployment for a number of members to whose character or conduct the Marion Manufacturing Company objected. The union considered this to be a discrimination in violation of the settlement, a contention to which the management would not agree.

Dissatisfaction of the union element grew, and during the night of October 1, a number of workers hastily struck. The mill, realizing that the strikers would attempt to prevent the day shift from coming in the next morning, gathered a band of deputies and the sheriffs outside the gates. As the day shift workers appeared, the strikers refused to obey the sheriff's orders that a way be cleared. The sheriff fired a tear-gas pistol, and in a moment was struggling with one of the strikers. Simultaneously, volleys of shots from the deputies were fired into the crowd of strikers. Bullet holes were later found in the mill behind the deputies, and some witnesses contend that strikers fired on the sheriff's party. At all events, six strikers were fatally wounded, four of them shot in the back, and fifteen other strikers received wounds. One deputy is said to have been grazed by a bullet. After this incident the mill immediately reopened and the strike was over, though over a hundred who were refused reëmployment had to be cared for by relief agencies—the Emergency Committee for Strikers' Relief, the Society of Friends, and trade union interests. The town stayed in some turmoil for months afterwards, with instances of arson and dynamiting occurring every now and then, and with a prolonged squabble as to the eligibility of trade unionists for membership in the East Marion Missionary Baptist Church.

There remained only a trial of Hoffman and a number of leaders and participants in the first strike on charges of riot and rebellion against the State of North Carolina, besides the trial of deputies accused of murder of strikers at the mill gate. The grand jury refused to include Sheriff Adkins in the indictment for murder. In the first trial, the charge of rebellion under a Carpet Bag statute of 1868, was disallowed by the judge, but Hoffman and three other unionists were convicted of resistance to law and sentenced. Hoffman was given thirty days in jail and a fine of $1,000, and the others were given six months in jail or at work on the roads—sentences from which appeal was taken, bail being allowed. In the murder trial, as at Gastonia, entirely conflicting accounts were given by the State and the defense, and the jury refused to convict.

The Marion strikes,[4] in particular the first one, illustrate the peculiar position in which the United Textile Workers is put by its refusal to endorse to the full strikes in which the participants have not been union members for as much as six months. The U. T. W. failing to take direct charge of the strike, worked mainly through leaders with whom it was not in complete agreement, but nevertheless shared in the aftermath of defeat. It was true also that the bitterness of the strikes was due in part to the unusual obstinacy of one of the companies. Conditions were, however, somewhat improved after the disturbance, the week being shortened, sewerage being laid in the village of the Marion Mill, and other concessions being made.

Three or four days after the beginning of the first strike at Elizabethton, a series of spontaneous strikes began to occur in South Carolina. Most of them concerned what the mill people called the "stretch-out," which involved increase of the number of machines tended by the operative, not always with satisfactory adjustment of wages. The strikes were unorganized and in some cases the workers definitely repudiated union leadership.

All of these strikes occurred in the Piedmont region. The first of these was at Ware Shoals, where on March 15, 1,200 workers left the plant spontaneously, in protest against certain features of the stretch-out. One of their first acts was to attempt to ride the efficiency expert out of town, but he had been forewarned and had already left. Otherwise the

[4] For a summary of the strikes, see Vol. VIII, No. 47, "The Strikes at Marion, North Carolina," of the *Information Service of the Department of Research and Education,* Federal Council of the Churches of Christ in America.

strike was orderly and was settled within ten days by the granting of the workers' demands. Before it was ended, however, 1,200 additional workers had come out at Pelzer, partly in sympathy with the Ware Shoals workers, and again in a demonstration against the stretch-out. The strikers, although entirely unorganized, elected a committee which interviewed the management, and the strikers returned after two days under an assurance of adjustments to be worked out in the near future.

Meanwhile the movement had spread to Greenville, where, at the end of March, three mills belonging to one company were struck. In another plant of the same company, at Woodruff, seven or eight hundred joined the original strikers a few days later. In the four mills involved the workers were in the main asking for the return to the system used before the stretch-out. The machinery of local committees and State conciliation was made use of by the workers and the company, but the strikers were persistent in calling for the entire ending of the stretch-out, and it was not until the strikes had lasted nearly two months that settlements were effected. Some unionism appeared in two of the plants, but it showed no strength and did not become an important issue. The settlement, when made, was not claimed as a victory by the strikers. Orderliness characterized all four strikes.[5]

Similar strikes occurred at Central and at Anderson. At Central, 750 workers took part in a completely victorious one-day strike against the stretch-out, March 29. Though unorganized, they had elected a committee, with which the mill dealt freely. Meanwhile the wave of strikes had spread

[5]Testimony of the president of the company concerned is to be found in Hearings before the Committee on Manufactures, United States Senate, on Senate Resolution 49, Working Conditions of the Textile Industry in North Carolina, South Carolina and Tennessee, May 8, 9, 20, 1919, pp. 112-129.

to Union, South Carolina. Here three mills went on strike between April 1 and 3, in each case the strikers demanding changes in the stretch-out. One strike was settled within two weeks by a signed agreement endorsing the stretch-out principle, praising harmony, and making no mention of unionism. In the other cases, settlement did not come until mid-May, when the mills granted a slight increase in wages. In the mill at Anderson, a strike of weavers, beginning on April 4, rapidly grew until there were over 1,000 out. Settlement was not reached for some weeks.

This whole series of spontaneous strikes was remarkable for the orderliness of the operatives, their prompt arranging for negotiations with the employers, the absence of important union organization, the willingness of employers to treat with strikers, and the frequency of partial victories.

In South Carolina the only strike in which the union entered to any extent was at Ware Shoals, three months after the first strike there had been settled. Some of the employes had been active in forming a U. T. W. local and when, early in July, two of these men were discharged, several hundred left the plant. Threats of violence to people who wished to go back to work induced the Governor to send two companies of guardsmen. The troops set up machine guns at the mill gates, and when the mill reopened nearly the full day and night shifts came in. The union, with only 200 members, was left with the problem of relief for over 800 people. It was thus defeated from the first, though it did not formally give in for seven weeks. The strikers remained orderly under trying circumstances; weeks after the strike was called off over 200 men were reported blacklisted and unable to find work.[6] What violence occurred was on the side of deputy sheriffs, who late in the

---

[6] Greensboro *Daily News*, Aug. 10, 1929.

strike forcibly carried two organizers out of the town.[7] The complete failure of this second dispute at Ware Shoals, where the union was involved, in contrast with the success of the first, can hardly have advanced the union's cause in the South Carolina Piedmont.

All of these strikes made it inevitable that a great new attempt should be made to organize in the cotton mills and indeed in the whole South. When the climax of the disturbance was scarcely past, the American Federation of Labor began its Toronto convention, in October 1929. Speeches before the convention by strikers from Elizabethton and Marion roused the labor men to a degree of fervor quite unusual, and plans were enthusiastically laid for following up the resolution of the year before.[8]

The venture of Southern organization was to be a cooperative one in which most of the component unions of the Federation were to share the burden of unionizing. The task of the American Federation of Labor was to be mainly coördinating the work of the hundred organizers whom the separate unions were to put into the field. Though each union was to give particular attention to its own craft, the services of all organizers were to be available for the textile workers. This campaign was actually launched in January, 1930, at a meeting of 200 delegates from all over the South at Charlotte, North Carolina.[9]

In the last two or three years, and particularly since the 1929 strikes, the union has met the beginnings of a change in Southern opinion. In 1927 appeared the first of a long succession of reports by Southern religious bodies on cotton mill conditions, all of them urging improvement, and most

[7] Columbia *State*, July 13, 1929.
[8] *Proc.*, American Federation of Labor, 1929, pp. 265-283.
[9] *American Federationist*, 37, No. 2, Feb., 1930, "Organize the South," William Green.

of them hinting at the desirability of organization of the workers. The press, though still decidedly "bourgeois," usually showed tolerance toward and in some instances advocacy of unionism. The impatience of the universities with the slow pace of progress had a striking illustration in the issuance of a demand for a survey of the industry, put out by a professor in the University of North Carolina and signed by four hundred prominent citizens of the State. Moreover, the union was able to reap a harvest of good will by the ever-present contrast of the methods and policies of the Communists. Southern manufacturers, long accustomed to call any trade unionist a Bolshevist, were taught a quick lesson in distinctions in the labor movement. The United Textile Workers emphasized especially in the South its program of union-management coöperation, which attracted favorable attention. On the whole, therefore, the U. T. W. had, in support from the general labor movement, and in a more responsive attitude on the part of the public, the best opportunity for Southern work in its history.

But so far as economic conditions went, the campaign was embarrassed by depression in the mills. The business slump in the preceding autumn had greatly lessened cotton consumption and even a program of severe curtailment in mill operation was unable to prevent overstocking of the market. In this situation, many mills were running only a few days a week. Widespread distress brought the total number of unemployed in North Carolina alone, in March, 1930, to 250,000.[10]

In spite of this, the efforts of the United Textile Workers began to meet response in the late spring. One of the first successes was at Danville, Virginia, where, after a wage reduction, the 4,500 operatives abandoned a company union

[10] New York *Times*, March 8, 1930.

which had been in existence for ten years and *en masse* joined the United Textile Workers. A running agitation for restoring the old wage and for introducing democratic coöperation of the union with the employer, has continued to this writing. Just south of Danville, at Leaksville, North Carolina, several hundreds of workers have been union members for some months. Nearby, in highly paternalistic mills at Greensboro, the issue of the right to organize is at present being wordily fought out. In all of these mills the Union has offered its help to the managements in scientific rearrangement of work schedules and in other problems of operation.[11] Farther South, substantial memberships have been built up at Greenville, at Columbus, Georgia, in Huntsville and Anniston, Alabama, and small locals to the number of some scores have been founded. So far as membership goes, however, it is doubtful if the Union has as yet had half the success it met by the end of the year 1919.

[11] *American Federationist,* 37, No. 5, May, 1930, pp. 542-3, "The New Unionism," Geoffrey C. Brown.

# CHAPTER IV

## CONCLUSIONS

IN REVIEWING the history of organizing efforts in the Southern textile mills since 1886, several hindrances and encouragements to unionism stand out. To consider the hindrances first:

The company-owned mill village has given the employer two sets of defenses. In the first place, he has been able to influence opinion toward the exclusion of union propaganda by means of a subtle pressure exerted through his welfare work and by virtue of his dominant economic position; fear of running counter to the employer's wishes, bound up with his ownership of the operative's house, prevents free expression of "disloyal sentiments." In the second place, if these barriers are overleaped and a union is formed in a given village, the employer has extraordinary resources in the way of mill-paid deputies, the right of eviction, prevention of trespass, influence over the churches through his monetary contributions to them, exclusion from welfare privileges, and control of meeting places.

Another obstacle to organization is the ignorance and farm background of most of the workers. Being relatively new to industry, large numbers of the operatives are still in the stage of reliance upon an employer rather than dependence upon autonomous collective action for economic safety. Contrary to much that has been said and printed, however, articulate loyalty to the employer is confined to a small group of influential villagers. Isolation on the farm and autocratic control in the mill villages have prevented the growth of the ordinary agencies of democratic participation in local affairs. This has meant unfamiliarity with the conduct of meetings, failure in estimating the quality of elected leaders, and difficulty in dealing collectively.

The reserve of labor on the farms, gradually pushing into factory employment, has kept the mills oversupplied with workers. This has been a manifest hindrance to union effort.

Poverty of the Southern operatives has been a principal discouragement. In the North the union has fought its dues up to a point where they now average about a dollar a month. This is a sum which the Southern operative can be induced to part with only in a cause devoutly believed in.

The union in the North has been weak. It has been able to finance Southern organizing on a large scale only at such times as it has had substantial help from the American Federation of Labor.

Enthusiasm of political authorities for industrial development has made them almost as intolerant as the mill owners toward interference with the factories' operation. This is true not only for the State but of individual cities and smaller communities, which fear that if the union becomes domiciled, new industries will not be attracted to the town. This has shown itself in a readiness to introduce troops upon slight provocation; troops have been used in more than a dozen places. It is noteworthy, however, that until 1929, injunctions had not been used with especial frequency in the South. Town councils have coöperated with mill managements to prevent parades and other union demonstrations. Another phase of this civic discouragement of unionism has been the distaste of the controlling commercial classes in each community for union activity. In town after town, local merchants, dependent on payrolls for their trade, have offered physical resistance to trade unionists.

Another difficulty has been the relative failure of the

union to enlist the support of the more respected people in the mill villages. This is not entirely the union's fault, for these individuals feel that they stand to benefit more from the favor of the employer. The union is at fault, however, to the extent to which it has sent down as organizers men whose character proved questionable. Some of the organizers whom the union has sent to the South have found themselves more at home in the bootleg fringe of the villages than with the better class of people.

Friends of the mills have originated and spread highly partisan anti-union propaganda. Charges of inefficiency and faithlessness on the part of the union, widely accepted by subordinate mill men and workers, have been persistently circulated.

In the matter of leadership, it is noteworthy that Southerners have latterly played a somewhat larger part in the textile union movement. Local leadership was important in the earliest Augusta unionism, and again in the 1898-1902 period of activity, and it appeared again in the North Carolina movement early in 1919. On the whole, however, the directing trade unionists have come from outside; a condition natural for unskilled and poorly educated workers, who universally have difficulty in finding competent leaders. However, the agitation in North Carolina in 1923-26, centering in Charlotte, was conducted by Southern men; the strikes at Elizabethton and Marion left much of the work in the hands of local operatives; the unorganized turn-outs in South Carolina last year were purely local in incentive; and the union movement in the non-textile trades has in the last four years showered personal as well as financial help both in the strikes and in the continuing organizing effort. An aggressive sectional consciousness is emerging in all the Southern State Federations of Labor. Workers' Education, which has lately carried scores of Southern mill operatives through labor colleges, to its enthusiasts promises trained Southern organizers who can head up the solidarity of the mill people.

In the middle ground, before turning to the encouragements to unionism in the South, the action of the courts has been fair on the whole. Lapse in the cases of Gastonia and Marion stands out in contrast to long years of legal encounters in which the union voiced little complaint.

In the matter of the Negro mill workers, who constitute about 10 per cent of the employes, the union has had no special difficulties. In four or five cases, colored locals have been formed, usually subordinate to the chartered white local, and attempts to discredit unionism through the race issue have failed.

On the favorable side the outstanding fact has been the readiness, in good times, of hundreds and often thousands of the mill workers to join the union, though this has not characterized every organizing attempt. The union has had at hand a ready-made solidarity of the mill people—in race, language, and religion—on which to build. At five definite periods the union has had marked success in signing membership—in 1886-7, 1898-1902, 1913-18, 1919-21, and 1929. Union organizers are agreed that women workers have joined as readily as men, and in strikes their fervor has often exceeded that of the men.

In strike after strike the newspapers have praised the patience and general peaceableness of the operatives. On the whole, the Southern workers in disputes have been careful of mill property and have respected legal authority. In the latter particular their forbearance and loyalty have been remarkable. This does not mean that the tradition of self-defense has been laid aside in industrial difference. Also, there has been aggression against strike breakers. Petty violence has accompanied most strikes.

Relative prosperity of the Southern industry, even at times of depression in the North, has been of powerful assistance. The workers have felt that money-making mills could be induced to grant better conditions and pay. The steady stream of Northern mills to the South has tended to keep down the labor surplus.

Until the last few years, middle class opinion in the South has been uniformly against organization of workers, but in the last epidemic of strikes a decided tendency to treat the union with tolerance and sometimes with encouragement has shown itself. A number of Southern journals have now assumed a distinctly liberal position on this question.

The rapid advance in education in the last decade has greatly helped the union's chances. Twenty years ago most union members signed with a mark; today nearly all are at least literate. It is still true, however, that the typical mill worker is hard to reach through the printed word.

While in the South the textile union has not had the advantage of a fully developed general labor movement, still the organized craftsmen in the region have contributed generously to textile strikes. This has occasionally had the accompanying feature of hesitance on the part of central labor unions and State federations of labor to agitate in the mills persistently. Many thousands of dollars have in the past been voted to textile strikes by these bodies, with discouraging results in the way of permanent organization. Help to textile workers is, however, on the increase.

In more cases than would ordinarily be believed, employers have been willing to accept conciliation. Special representatives of the State governors and conciliators from the

Department of Labor have helped to settle a score of strikes in the textile South.

Until recently the United Textile Workers had in the South the free field which obtained nowhere else. Attempts of dissentient textile unions to organize in the South have been negligible. It does not appear that the Communist entry of 1929 will offer continuing difficulty.

# INDEX